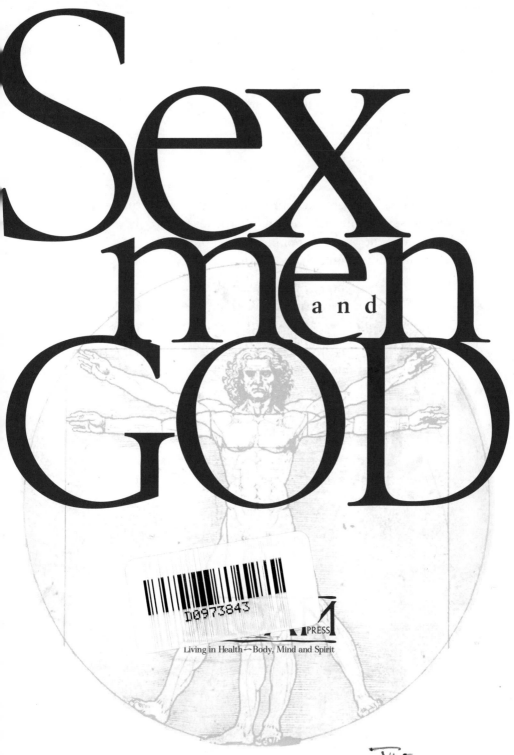

Sex
men
and
GOD

PRESS
Living in Health--Body, Mind and Spirit

Douglas Weiss

Sex, Men and God by Douglas Weiss
Published by Siloam Press
A part of Strang Communications Company
600 Rinehart Road
Lake Mary, Florida 32746
www.siloampress.com

Unless otherwise noted, all Scripture quotations are from the Holy Bible, New International Version. Copyright © 1973, 1978, 1984, International Bible Society. Used by permission.

Scripture quotations marked KJV are from the King James Version of the Bible.

Scripture quotations marked NKJV are from the New King James Version of the Bible. Copyright © 1979, 1980, 1982 by Thomas Nelson, Inc., publishers. Used by permission.

Author's Note: The testimonies of individuals in this book are fictitious and created from composites of clients who share similar issues. Names and identifying information have been changed to protect confidentiality. Any similarities between the names and stories of individuals described in this book and individuals known to readers is coincidental and not intentioned.

Cover design by Rachel Campbell

Library of Congress Catalog Card Number: 2002103096
International Standard Book Number: 0-88419-881-2

02 03 04 05   8765432

Printed in the United States of America

*Dedicated to the strong, the broken,
the pure and not so pure—to all who
are blessed to be men*

Contents

INTRODUCTION

I believe that God wants every Christian man to be sexually successful. He desires all of us to enter into the holy of holies where spirit, soul and body intimacy occurs with your wife on a regular basis. His desire is to equip each one of us with the skills to be spiritually and emotionally intimate outside of the bedroom so that we can be sexually successful inside of the bedroom.

Are you wondering what a sexually successful man is and how you can become one? I am asked this question, along with many others, when I tell people that I am writing a book about men experiencing successful sexuality.

Let me be perfectly clear. Sex is by far one of God's best ideas! Don't you agree? I imagine the Creator could have made procreation a behavior that brought little pleasure and only engaged our bodies, completely detached from the wealth of a soul and spirit experience. What a bummer sex would have been if that were the case.

Thankfully our Maker decided to be very creative concerning our sexuality. Not only does your body go through the greatest physiological changes, but when engaging successfully in sex you also experience the highest chemical reward possible for your body.

As a therapist, I have counseled with thousands of men regarding sexuality issues. During this time, I have learned that many men are not sexually successful. I have "clocked in" years of my life listening to men as they share varied stories of their lack of sexual success. These men and their wives want to be sexually successful, but even after several decades of marriage, they have not achieved sexual success.

Why haven't many men experienced sexual success? Although there are different answers to that question, there are several broad sexual deficits that have commonality among many men.

The first deficit stems from the fact that many men have never received reliable information about true sexuality from their fathers. While traveling the country speaking at men's conferences, I often ask men how long their sex talk with their fathers lasted. Over 95 percent of the men questioned stated that it was less than three minutes long. You can understand how such a deficit of information from a sexual expert—your dad—would force you to launch your own quest to discover successful sexuality.

The second-largest deficit perpetrating the lack of sexual success is the source from which most young men acquire their sexual information. For boys fourteen to sixteen years of age their main source for sexual information is usually other fourteen- to sixteen-year-old boys. They may never have had sex, but they lie about that also. For many young men today, pornographic literature, the mainstream media, prime-time sitcoms, movies, magazines and, more recently, the Internet are primary sources for learning about sexuality.

The good news is that regardless of whatever deficit of information you have suffered in your past, you can have a phenomenal three-dimensional sex life that will reach a plane of sexual success and satisfaction you never thought possible.

Like many men, I was misinformed early on about sexuality, and I had experiences that could have kept me from sexual success. But I kept searching until I found the information that we must have in order to become sexually successful and to maintain that success throughout life!

On the following pages you will be exposed to principles

and information that can bring you to sexual success. Once you experience sexuality as God intended it, you will never be able to settle for less again—I guarantee it! It is an incredible journey that offers awesome rewards.

This journey, which I call *Sex, Men and God*, involves a process—there is no magic bullet. If you choose the process, ahead of you lies a journey during which equipping, informing and for many, healing will take place. When you reach the end of this journey you will be a sexually successful man who can be fearless in prayer, a threat to the enemy of our souls and a spiritual blessing to your wife, family, church and community.

ONE

Internal and External Sexuality

During our journey to successful sexuality, we will travel through many difficult areas and visit many facets of male sexuality. In order to navigate effectively these difficult areas and successfully reach our journey's end, we need to remember that all of our discussion involves God's divine design for men. God's gift to men is our sexuality. It is a divine gift that we have from birth to death. Yet, as men, we are misunderstood many times because of our God-given desire to consummate our marriage regularly.

I also believe that when men appropriately understand their sexuality they will experience three-dimensional sexuality that is wonderful and productive. The ability to connect with your spouse in three God-given dimensions—spirit, soul and body—can satisfy you so profoundly that you do not even desire sex the next day. Imagine being that sexually satiated on a regular basis; that is sexual success!

Realizing the value of your sexuality will help you avoid the pitfalls of misusing it—pitfalls that result in damaging yourself, your relationship with God and even future generations. That is why we have presented these chapters in *Sex, Men and God* to address the many magnificent facets of our sexuality—to give you the keys to understanding the value of your sexuality.

The enemy of our soul has concentrated his attacks against God's gift of male sexuality. He is fully aware that this gift, if misunderstood or misused, can lead to consequences that extend through family lines for generations to come. Likewise, God knows the blessing of a man of God who understands his sexuality and submits it to the lordship of Christ. The blessing of a sexually healthy man also impacts his sons and daughters for generations.

God's gift to men is our sexuality.

Understanding that male sexuality is God's great design can motivate every man to exert whatever effort is required to complete his personal journey to sexual success. God offers to every man who chooses to complete this journey the wonderful reward of sexual success. Perhaps you are not sure yet what that goal looks like. You are about to discover God's gift to you from His perspective.

I have studied the Scriptures for almost twenty years and have clearly seen that God's Word addresses what I call the two sides of sexuality. By this I mean that He clearly communicates the reality of our external sexuality as well as our internal sexuality.

EXTERNAL SEXUALITY

By the term *external sexuality* I refer to the actual sexual acts that you participate in with your physical body. These sex acts fall basically into two categories. The first category is comprised of sex acts approved by God in the context of a monogamous relationship with your wife. The second category includes sex acts that are disapproved and discouraged by God. These include sexual acts with anyone prior to marriage and outside of marriage.

In Scripture, God is very clear about sex acts of which He does not approve. When He wrote the Ten Commandments to His people, He stated clearly, "You shall not commit adultery" (Exod. 20:14). And He doesn't mince words in describing how committing adultery leads to death. (See Proverbs 5.)

For the expanded version of what God does *not* want us to do with our external sexuality, we have only to read Leviticus 18. (Please turn to Appendix A and read this awesome list of shall-nots given to us by our Creator.)

Some of you may object to this exhaustive list of shall-nots by saying, "That's the Old Testament." The truth is that both the Old Testament and the New Testament express God's heart for us to be sexually pure. God is clear throughout Scripture that He intends external sexuality to be reserved only for your wife. His concern is for your happiness as well as your wife's happiness. I personally think God has received a bad rap for communicating His loving concern about our sexual behavior.

As a sex therapist, I think I have heard about every sexual exploit listed in Leviticus 18 being committed by men who call themselves Christians. But I also hear of the tremendous guilt and shame, often suffered for decades, that participating in these shall-nots caused them.

God isn't against sexual fun, but He is against us hurting ourselves by misusing the gift of sexuality. I have never counseled anyone who has not felt some pain as a result of breaking God's perfect design for sexuality. God is love (1 John 4:16). He expects love to motivate us so that we can have the absolute best sex of our lives.

I know that some of you reading this book may be feeling some regret over your past sexual behavior. Jesus came to set us free from all of our sin, including sexual sin. In our journey together, I will walk with you down the path that will allow you to heal in this area. I know from experience that Jesus can heal, restore and give you sexual success all the days of your life.

In the New Testament the apostle Paul reveals more about God's warning to us to avoid all sexual immorality. He states clearly, "The acts of the sinful nature are obvious: sexual immorality, impurity and debauchery . . . orgies, and the like . . . those who live like this will not inherit the kingdom of God" (Gal. 5:19–21). This is strong New Testament language about external sexuality.

We read similar exhortations in other New Testament passages, including Romans 1, which describes God's judgments for wrongdoing, and Revelation 2, which exposes the false prophetess Jezebel who is leading church members into sexual immorality.

God isn't against sexual fun, but He is against us hurting ourselves by misusing the gift of sexuality.

Sexual practices outside of marriage are wrong from God's perspective in both the Old and New Testaments. Of course, we know this; it has been preached for at least two centuries by Catholics as well as Protestants, and especially within evangelical or nondenominational Bible churches. So I won't belabor this biblical understanding because it may be so familiar that you actually tune it out. Like a song you have heard over and over again, this biblical message of morality can seem like background music you don't notice anymore.

Tuning out is especially true for Christian men who grew up in church youth groups. They heard the message of "don't touch the girls" too often. They got the message and don't need to hear it again. But these young men only heard or understood God's Word as it applied to *external* sexuality. While they knew they couldn't touch the girls, they believed that they certainly could look and not get into trouble. As long as the outside appearance was OK, they thought they could do whatever they wanted on the inside. This faulty understanding has created a duality in Christian men that keeps them from becoming sexually successful. For this reason, we need to gain a clear understanding of the other side of sexuality—internal sexuality.

INTERNAL SEXUALITY

Internal sexuality involves your sexual feelings, thoughts, fantasies and impulses. Internal sexuality is what you do with your eyes, your heart and your creative mind. This side of sexuality is also a gift from God.

This internal dimension of your sexuality can function undetected by those around you. You can lust after another woman's body without anyone knowing or condemning. At least that's what many of the Christian men I have talked to believed in adolescence. They rationalized that as long as they only looked and didn't touch, they were good boys.

As adults this now may sound immature, but when you're a fourteen- or sixteen-year-old, this faulty reasoning is to be expected. The problem is that some men remain stuck at that level of thinking all of their lives because neither they nor their spiritual leaders have adequately addressed the important issue of their internal sexuality.

DON'T COVET HER.

To begin to address this issue, let's return to the backbone of our faith—the Ten Commandments. We have already discussed Exodus 20:14: "You shall not commit adultery." Now let's scroll down to the last commandment: "You shall not covet your neighbor's wife" (Exod. 20:17). This mandate deals with our *internal* sexuality.

God does not want us to lust, covet or sexually desire our neighbor's wife. I can imagine that some of you are already thinking, *Well, I have six neighbors on my street, and I don't lust after or covet them, so I'm OK.* That's not the point.

Jesus did a great job defining who our neighbors really are in the story of the Good Samaritan. (See Luke 10:25–37.) When you read the parable, you will rightly conclude that from God's perspective a neighbor includes everyone.

You may still try to rationalize, *OK, if a woman is married, then I should be a good boy and not lust after her.* According to that reasoning, you may still think it's acceptable to lust after single and divorced women. Not exactly—almost every woman you meet will be a man's wife someday. So, the bottom line: Don't lust after *any* woman. Other scriptures back up this point, making it obvious that lust is indeed sin. It is wrong. (See Colossians 3:5–6; 1 Peter 4:3–5; 1 John 2:16.)

THE RIGHT WAY

The apostle Paul wrote to Timothy concerning a Christian man's right relationship with women: "Treat . . . older women as mothers, and younger women as sisters, with absolute purity" (1 Tim. 5:1–2). Can you imagine lusting after your mom or sister? All women are sisters or mothers and children of God our Father. They deserve to be treated with absolute purity. Therefore, lusting after *any* woman as a sex object is undesirable and sinful in God's eyes.

Yes, you may notice an attractive woman, but to make a sex object out of her by continuing to check her out is wrong. Lust is a powerful enemy to your sexual success. It can lead you into all the wrong places. The apostle James warns us of the destructive power of lust: "Then, after desire [lust] has conceived, it gives birth to sin; and sin, when it is full-grown, gives birth to death" (James 1:15).

I have seen this "death" progression in thousands of lives. The lust often begins in one's teen years and gradually spawns into behaviors such as viewing porn, fantasizing and masturbating. These practices continue into marriage.

While they can go unnoticed by others, they leave the man indulging in them spiritually impotent (dead). What started simply as lust of the eye becomes a full-blown lifestyle of secret sin. Secret or not, sin does have consequences.

More often than not, those consequences include a husband losing his relationship with his wife and family. I have seen this lived out over and over again. Lust, sin and death are a straight continuum that is inevitable unless the man turns his heart to God.

I like to compare lust to an apple seed. Inside that little seed is the map to create an entire apple tree. It cannot happen instantly, and conditions must be favorable, but when that map is followed, an apple tree will be the inevitable result. Lust works in that same way. Your soul, which includes your mind, will and emotions, is the fertile soil in which the seed of lust grows. You plant that seed, and you continue to "nourish" it and water it. Then *whammo*! Over time you reap the sin and death that were part of the map inside of the seed of lust. Remember that lust is an *internal* sexuality issue that must be distinguished from other sexual issues in order to achieve long-term sexual success.

Lust is a powerful enemy to your sexual success.

If you truly understand how powerful this little seed of lust is, you will see why the Bible encourages us to run from it. The apostle Paul exhorted Timothy, "Flee also youthful lusts; but pursue righteousness, faith, love, peace with those who call on the Lord out of a pure heart" (2 Tim. 2:22, NKJV). God knows the power that the seed of lust holds. That is why Scripture warns us: "Do not lust in your heart after her beauty or let her captivate you with her eyes" (Prov. 6:25).

Although others may not be able to see you lust, God does, and you will have to answer before Him for using your mind and time in this manner. Women are not on the planet for you to access their beauty by your standards. They are not to be scanned into your mind or heart in order to fantasize. Women are people, and more importantly, they are God's people. He does not condone lust, and we shouldn't either.

TIPS ON OVERCOMING LUST

I wrote a book several years ago titled *101 Freedom Exercises: A Christian Guide for Sexual Addiction Recovery.* In it I outlined several exercises to help men get free and stay free from lust. The following is a summarization of some of these exercises, as well as a few more I have learned along the way.

PRAY FOR THEM.

I personally have used this one successfully for years. When a person becomes an object of lust for you, you can turn her back into a person by giving her a relational context to God and others in prayer. Here is a sample prayer:

> God, I know You love this woman, that You died for her and that You desire a relationship with her. I pray that if she doesn't know You, You will reveal Yourself to her so she can know You for eternity. I pray that her husband (or future husband) will be a man of God, full of Your Spirit and wisdom. I pray that her children (or future children) will know and serve You all their days. I pray that You would encourage her parents and bless their daughter. Amen.

Now how many women do you think the enemy is going to present to you to lust after if all you do is pray them into the kingdom? Early on the self-defense arts teach you how to block a punch that is thrown at you. When the enemy throws you a temptation, you can block it by praying—and you will walk away feeling successful instead of guilty.

LOOK THEM IN THE EYES.

If you lust after a woman below the neck or waist, then keep your eyes above the neck so they don't travel over her body scanning her. If you start to lust after women when you gaze into their eyes, avoid their eyes as well.

FOLLOW THE ONE-TO-THREE-SECOND RULE.

In sex addiction recovery, there is a three-second policy: Don't look at a woman longer than three seconds. Living today in the high-speed television and computer age, men can learn to scan a woman in less time than that. Regardless, keep your gaze very short. And remember, you aren't under any obligation to check out each woman that walks by.

ESTABLISH ACCOUNTABILITY.

I find that if a man walks in the light in the area of lust, he is less likely to struggle. That means exposing the hidden aspect of your internal sexuality involved in lust. James 5:16 says, "Confess your sins to each other and pray for each other so that you may be healed." It's great to confess your sin of lust to Jesus, for He will always forgive you (1 John 1:9). But most of us who struggle with lust don't need only forgiveness; we need *healing*. The Scriptures clearly state that healing comes when we humble ourselves to one another, confessing our sin and praying for each other.

Don't wimp out and try to do this with your wife only. Something powerful happens when you humble yourself to another man. I purposely say "man." Man to man, be honest with a brother in the Lord, and you will see lust decrease tremendously. Having an accountability partner like this can help you eliminate the seed of lust that would otherwise bring a future harvest of sin and death. Accountability works! (See Ecclesiastes 4:10.)

KEEP A LUST LOG.

Some men in an accountability relationship keep a *lust log*. This is simply a piece of paper you keep in your pocket.

Each time you lust or objectify a woman, put a mark on the paper. Check in daily for one hundred days with your accountability partner as to how you are doing.

Some competitive friends even make the man with the highest score pay for the lunch of the low-scoring man each week. You'll be amazed at how quickly you can stop lusting when there is free food on the line!

If you are still doubtful, it may be that you do not understand that lust is a learned, intentional behavior. Because that is true, it is possible to unlearn lust and choose not to allow it. Filling your mind with the divine power of God's Word is one of the greatest weapons to use to overcome lust. Here are a few of my favorite weapons:

> Put to death [or mortify], therefore, whatever belongs to your earthly nature: sexual immorality, impurity, lust, evil desires.
>
> —COLOSSIANS 3:5

> So I say, live by the Spirit, and you will not gratify the desires of the sinful nature.
>
> —GALATIANS 5:16

> Do not conform any longer to the pattern of this world, but be transformed by the renewing of your mind.
>
> —ROMANS 12:2

> Praise be to the God and Father of our Lord Jesus Christ! In his great mercy he has given us new birth into a living hope through the resurrection of Jesus Christ from the dead, and into an inheritance that can never perish, spoil or fade—kept in heaven for you, who through faith are shielded by God's power.
>
> —1 PETER 1:3–5

KILL IT!

Well, how exactly do you put to death your earthly nature? Ted Haggard, my pastor at New Life Church in

Colorado Springs, has a great way of explaining how he kills himself every morning. He gets in the prayer closet and asks God to strangle anything of his flesh, to destroy any sin patterns today. He asks God to fill him with the fruit of the Spirit, the fear of the Lord and the power and might described in Isaiah chapter 11. I think it's a great idea. I do this regularly, too.

From our discussion, I think you get the picture that God is concerned about both sides of our sexuality: our external sexual behavior and our internal sexual beliefs. It is God's desire for every Christian man to have sexual success. And it is my desire for you as well. I enjoy being made in God's image, which includes my sexuality. I want to honor God with all of myself, and I know you do, too.

In order to achieve that, as we continue our journey, we are going to explore the territory of this divine gift called male sexuality. The journey's terrain will change with every chapter. When you complete the journey, however, I think you will be able to personally connect with the integration of sex, men and God for your personal sexual success. You will understand how these three—sex, men and God—can live together in unity and harmony, giving you the ability to become a powerful man of God who will impact your generation as well as those who follow you.

TWO

The Sexual Brain

The human creation was a marvelous idea. God took so much time and creativity in making our bodies that it would take volumes to begin to explain the beauty, complexity and all of the miracles contained in the physical body. This marvel is no truer than in the aspect of male sexuality.

> I praise you because I am fearfully and wonderfully made.
>
> —PSALM 139:14

Changes occur in the male physical body during the sexual act that not only change its physical appearance, but also affect it physiologically in many ways when a man is being sexual. In this chapter, I will walk you through a very important aspect of some of the physiological changes that occur in the male brain during a sexual release. This information will be very helpful to you in becoming more sexually successful in your marriage and will also help any healing process that needs to take place from your past.

To be a sexually successful man, you must have a sexually

successful brain. Typically what a man thinks about and focuses on is what he ends up doing. For example, many men have spent money and time studying books about financial success, health or spiritual growth and, after practicing the principles and techniques involved, have eventually obtained the goal.

You need to understand the significance of the brain to your sexuality.

And yet, while all the case studies confirm that men spend time thinking about sex many times throughout the day, we must ask the question why so many men are not having sexual success. I believe one reason is because of the manner in which men are thinking about sex. Another reason is the way men's brains have actually been trained about sex. This faulty thinking and training impedes the sexual success that men could experience. The good news is that there is an answer for these problems. It is possible to create a sexually successful brain. (We will address the issue of retraining the brain in chapter seven.)

First, you need to understand the significance of the brain to your sexuality. The lack of understanding of the role of the brain in your sexuality is by far one of the greatest gaps in a man's sexual education. For that reason it is necessary to make this aspect of sexuality a priority in our discussion on sexual success.

To begin our discussion, let's review a classic experiment. In college you may have learned about a man named Ivan Petrovich Pavlov, whose experimentation led to a groundbreaking theory called *classical conditioning*. In Pavlov's experiment, he rang a bell and then fed his dog some food. The dog began to associate food with the sound of the bell and salivated whenever it heard the bell ring. The dog's reaction was a conditioned, or learned, response to the stimulus—the ringing bell. The principle of classical conditioning basically means that when you ring the bell, the dog expects to be fed.

This principle is very important to our subject of the sexual brain. When Pavlov's dog heard the bell and anticipated the reward, a neurological response was triggered and the dog salivated, preparing his body for food. The male brain goes through a similar process when a man desires sex. During sex, chemicals called endorphins and enkephalins rush to the excitement center (preoptic neuron) of a man's brain, filling it to the highest possible level. The result is a "reward" of sorts. Not even a "runner's high" compares to this feeling!

The preoptic neuron is the section of the brain where excitement and risk are experienced. Men who take risks such as skydiving, bungee jumping or deep-sea diving utilize the same part of the brain as sex does. However, sex, by far, produces the greatest chemical release, making his brain and body feel their absolute best. That's why men love sex and why it's so appealing. Sex provides the big enchilada for your brain!

SEX GLUE

As mentioned earlier, when a man ejaculates, his brain receives its maximum chemical reward. Critical to a man's sexual success is understanding that whatever he *looks* at while having an ejaculation is what he will sexually connect or "glue" to. Whatever his eyes focus on when he sexually releases—a person, image or object—will become etched in his brain as a photographic attachment toward that person, image or object. I call it "sex glue." After a period of time having sex with the same person, when he sees her, he is going to feel attached to her.

Isn't it just like God to design something that would

make you totally happy with the wife He designed for you? This is the original thought God had in mind with this process—that as a man you would obey His Word and not have sex until marriage. Then after marriage you would start having sexual releases, just with her. And when you look at her during a sexual experience, *wham!* You are glued to her. Over a short period of time she becomes your only chemical reinforcement for your sexual experience, and you are totally happy with her regardless of her height, weight or proportions.

Unfortunately, most men reading this book may not have experienced sex in this satisfying way that God intended. They have initiated their own quest for sexual success and have suffered the consequences.

I want to share with you some of those consequences from stories of clients I had the privilege of counseling. The first is Stan, a forty-eight-year-old self-employed man. The second is Tom, who was a thirty-eight-year-old corporate professional making $300,000 a year.

When Stan was a teenager he lived on a farm with his family. He reached adolescence with the normal sexual desires. Then, when he was in his teens, he began to be sexual with himself. The bed he slept on in his parent's house had uneven legs, so as Stan was masturbating, his bed would go bump, bump, bump. The sound was heard throughout the house. The next morning Stan's family would laugh and joke about his behavior the night before.

You have heard the cliché that necessity is the mother of invention. Stan, a smart farm boy, found a solution to his embarrassment relatively quickly. He waited until everyone in the house was asleep. Then he put his boots on and walked quietly out of the house, through the yard and past the barn where no one could see him.

While being sexual with himself, Stan had the choice of looking up or down. He chose to look down. The boots he was wearing were in his field of vision. Do you remember

Pavlov's theory of ringing the bell and feeding the dog? You guessed it: Stan began to connect his sexual release to his boots. When Stan finally called for help, he was forty-eight years old. He had never masturbated or had sex with a woman without his boots on. And he had a full wall for his boot collection. This is a true story of a man whose sex glue attached to the wrong thing.

∾

Tom is a corporate climber who trained his brain for sex while viewing pornography. Tom had a particular habit with pornography that is different from most. He used to cut off one of the woman's legs in the picture or take a black marker and scribble over one of the legs. Throughout his teenage years and adulthood he continued this behavior of masturbating to one-legged women.

Tom, being an attractive guy, married an extremely attractive woman. His wife could easily have been a model. Tom, however, didn't want to have sex with her. Why not? Because she had two legs! Tom's sex glue connected to one-legged women. He had no desire for his beautiful two-legged wife. Remember: Ring the bell, feed the dog. Even though one's habits don't seem to make sense, the sex glue they produce is real.

The sexual conditioning of your brain is probably one of the greatest determining factors to your ultimate sexual success as a Christian man. Fortunately, after receiving counseling, Tom is back on track and applying the principles of this book to his sexuality. He and his brain now desire to have sex with his beautiful wife.

∾

These are only two examples of the many things to which men have become sexually attached that rob them of the possibility of being sexually successful. They serve to illustrate that the "ring the bell, feed the dog theory" functions indiscriminately, affecting even Christians. It is simply a fact that consistent viewing of anything or anyone during a sexual experience creates a sexual desire for that object or person.

Sadly, many men have badly trained their brain hundreds or thousands of times by being sexual with themselves before their first legitimate sexual encounter. How have you trained your brain?

SEXUAL CONDITIONING

If you were sexual as a teenager, you created a pathway in your brain for a sexual attachment. You probably chose one of several options for that pathway from these four major categories: images, fantasy, people and objects. Before we explain the different brain pathways that can be created, we need to define briefly these four categories that established your sexual conditioning.

OPTION 1—IMAGES

Many teenagers have clocked in hundreds of hours reinforcing their sexuality with images from pornography. Teens who don't have access to pornography often view lingerie catalogs. Adult men spend countless hours viewing pornography in magazines or on the Internet. Thus they have created a neuro-pathway that craves such images for its satisfaction.

OPTION 2—FANTASIES

Some young men, not having access to pornography, did what they thought was the next best thing—they made up their own fantasy images for their sexual stimulation, which can be limitless. They may have imagined people they knew or people they wish they knew and placed them in their fantasy world. Some have created infinite encounters that include a myriad of sexual behaviors. This type of sexual conditioning can be combined with images, or it can solely involve fantasy.

OPTION 3—OBJECTS

Some men's sexual conditioning connected them to specific clothing or other objects. Others were conditioned sexually by connecting to a woman's body as an object without connecting to her as a person. These men engage in one-night-stands or solicit prostitutes. They condition their sexuality in an object-type manner. They believe sex is not about relationships, but about objects.

OPTION 4—PEOPLE

Some men experienced sex for the first time and thereafter in a healthy monogamous relationship. In their conditioning process they connected to a person who cared for them, and sex was a part of their relationship. Sex for them was more about "connecting" and not just the act of sex.

You can see how one man's sexual conditioning experience can be very different from someone else's. Some men were involved in their sexual conditioning before becoming a Christian, others not until after they were saved. Sexual conditioning explains why some men have sexual fetishes, preferences and desires. Any sexual behavior combined with repetitive conditioning can become a sexual choice for you.

Now that you understand better the principle of "ring the bell, feed the dog," you can also understand that anything can become the "bell." Depending on your sexual conditioning, pornography, fantasy, people and objects will become the "bell" for you. Any teenager, knowingly or unknowingly, can establish a sexually successful brain or a sexually distracted brain.

BRAIN PATHWAYS

I have been studying for many years the brain pathways men have created through their sexual conditioning. After I explain each pathway, I will give you the formula for discovering what your pathway is.

Before I begin, I want to encourage you that no matter

how you have developed your brain, you can still learn how to retrain your brain to be as sexually successful as you desire. Christ meets you where you are—even sexually. He then gives you His Spirit and wisdom to retrain your brain so that you can give Him glory.

BRAIN 1—THE UNI-FOCUSED BRAIN

During adolescence, a teenager's brain is typically quite undistracted. If the teen begins to masturbate during adolescence and continues into young adulthood without ever creating a fantasy world or using pornography or other stimuli for attachment or nurturing, then he basically masturbates with no feelings of guilt or shame involved.

This person may have sexual encounters prior to marriage as well, but the encounters are characterized by a more or less loving relationship. The stimulus of the brain is usually monogamous in this relationship.

When this man marries, most likely he intuitively has sex in a connected manner. Sex for this man is relational, sensual and intense. He stays monogamous, and if he does masturbate, it is occasional, never compulsive, and is not connected to anything. Here is what this brain looks like during pre-marriage and post-marriage:

DIAGRAM 1

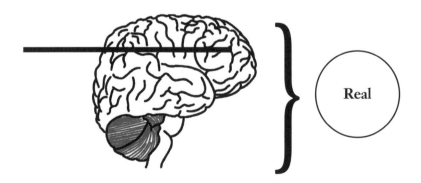

Notice that the thickness of the pathway for this neurological reinforcement is huge, creating the possibility for the most intense sexual satisfaction. Such a brain has been reinforced by one "bell": that of his wife. When this man's brain thinks about "sex," it thinks of the woman with whom he has had a long-term, monogamous relationship. His brain is very satisfied with his sex life because he is satisfied with his wife relationally and physically. This man may notice other women, but he is totally satisfied sexually by his monogamous relationship. She may or may not be attractive to others, but to him, she is the most attractive woman alive.

This man's brain has little to no sexual distractions. It allows the owner the time to focus on the other aspects of his life, as he deems necessary. This man is most likely to stay monogamous. Just as some men intuitively understand wealth, health and other important issues in life, the owner of this brain is, in all probability, intuitively sexually successful.

BRAIN 2—THE DUAL-FOCUSED BRAIN

The dual-focused brain often develops during adolescence due to sexual reinforcement behavior. It begins when a teen masturbates and at the same time views pornography, engages in fantasy or attaches to an object. The person with a dual-focused brain typically has a habit of masturbation, the frequency of which is quite regular during adolescence and early adulthood and coincides with connecting to something other than a person.

During adolescence, sexual experimentation overall is usually nonrelational. In order for this man's brain to initiate an orgasm, he has to move into a disconnected state with an object, fantasy or pornography. He may have had periods of recreational sex during adolescence, but his brain will primarily be sexually conditioning him to prefer fantasy, pornography, objects or the use of people as objects.

DIAGRAM 2

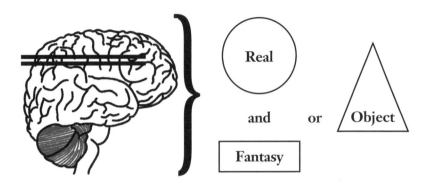

Notice in diagram 2 that this man's neuro-pathway is split. He doesn't receive the intensity that a uni-focused brain can experience. During marriage the person with such a brain is usually not content. Sex with his wife becomes less than exciting due to his inability to be intimate or solely conditioned sexually toward his wife. He often will complain about sex or her "imperfect body." This man's brain will usually maintain dual sexuality, of which his wife may or may not be aware.

He may be having a secret life of masturbation with the involvement of pornography, fantasy or objects. This man may technically not be having sex with others, but his sexuality is definitely split. If, however, his brain has the opportunity to fulfill its fantasy, the urge to give in to that behavior in the future can be overwhelming.

BRAIN 3—THE MULTI-FOCUSED BRAIN

In my professional experience, I have never counseled a man with a multi-focused brain who has said he experiences sexual contentment. During adolescence, his brain has no guidelines whatsoever. He masturbates regularly and compulsively. His brain may have chemical imbalances or psychological deficits. His sexual release is a means by which he is compensating for or trying to balance such deficits as depression or bipolar disorders.

During adolescence, his brain often attaches to three of the four sexual conditioning behaviors: fantasy, pornography, objects or the use of people as objects. He utilizes any of these to get his sexual "fix." For this man's brain it's all about sex. If he experiences emotional intimacy during sex, it will be sporadic or rare.

DIAGRAM 3

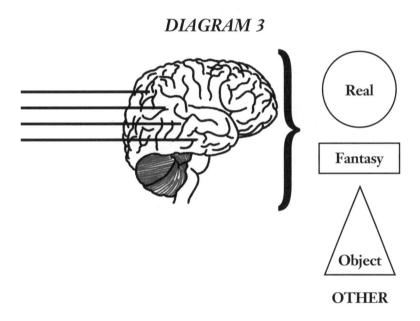

Notice that this profile of a man's brain is by far the most sexually fractured. The man with the multi-focused brain often has difficulty in marriage and other relationships. He believes the world is all about getting his needs met. This man can function at work, but he is often working or earning far beneath his potential. If he develops a monogamous relationship, intimacy is often difficult throughout the entire span of the relationship.

This man may engage in sexual behavior outside of his marriage relationship, but he doesn't see anything wrong with this because he believes everyone else is doing it. He considers that it was "only sex." More than likely, this man struggled within his family of origin and has experienced sexual abuse, sexual addictions or sexual anorexia (which I'll discuss later).

This man is also very defensive when talking about his objects of sexual pleasure because his brain has become dependent on the chemical high it experiences combined with the altered state he has created during his sexual release. Discussing the negative effects of his behavior with him could have explosive results.

UNDERSTANDING YOUR *BRAIN*

As you can see from the above discussion, not all men have the same sexual brain. Your brain pathway, created by the sexual conditioning it has received, predetermines your interior sexual belief and affects your external sexuality. For example, the sexually uni-focused brain will tend toward monogamy and will receive the best sex within a monogamous relationship for life.

The dual-focused brain is often torn between conservative sexuality and whatever his pornographic consumption dictates to him. He often feels that if he could have this type of sexuality, then he would really be happy. He experiences less satisfaction in marriage than the man with the sexually uni-focused brain because of this split in focus.

The multi-focused brain is not concerned with long-term happiness. Happiness for this man exists only for the moment. The adventure is an experiment with a new object. He has by far the most liberal sexual beliefs, and any attempt at compromise would be seen as a personal attack against his individual rights.

You can see how your brain and its sexual conditioning not only dictate your neurological preference and your current sexual appetite, but also your psychological and philosophical paradigm about sexuality. It is very important to realize that previous sexual conditioning lays the foundation for your current sexual paradigms.

This discussion comes early in this book because as you travel the road to sexual success, some of your neurologically reinforced paradigms—your "ring the bell, feed the dog" habits—are going to jump right out at you. They have created a neuro-pathway in your brain connecting the object to the pleasure. Be prepared for this to happen as you continue reading.

WHAT KIND OF BRAIN DO YOU HAVE?

Great question! I get asked this question all the time in my office in Colorado. When you understand your brain, you truly can understand yourself sexually to a much greater degree. As you read, always remember, the good news is that you can retrain your brain for sexual success. It is just like the man who struggled with finances. If he can learn the principles of wealth, he can learn to gain wealth for himself and his family.

Some of you are about to journey to a place so private that you may want to write your thoughts, known only to you, on a separate piece of paper. First, you'll need to compile a sexual reinforcement history This neurological road map will give you necessary details regarding the present status of your sexual brain.

The good news is that you can retrain your brain for sexual success.

In the chart below or on a separate piece of paper, fill out the information that's requested. We will walk together through the interpretation of this data in a moment.

Sexual Conditioning Chart A

Age	Total masturbation per week or month (i.e., 2x/wk, 1x/mo.)	Total relational sexual encounters per week or month
10–15		
15–20		
21–25		
26–30		
31–35		
36–40		
41–45		
46–50		
51–55		
56–60		
61–65		
66+		

After you choose a frequency (for example, two times per week) of how often you have masturbated, then follow this formula to get your total for a five-year period. If you masturbated two times per week, multiply 2 x 260 (52 weeks x 5 years), which gives you a grand total of 520 times that you have masturbated for the period of five years. If you are using months, (i.e., two times per month) then use the monthly formula for your total. Multiply 2 x 60 (12 months x 5 years). This will give you a grand total of 120. Be honest. Only you are looking at these numbers.

Using Chart B we are going to look further at your masturbating and sex behaviors in order to hone in on your particular range of sexual conditioning. Using the numbers from Chart A, write down your estimate.

Sexual Conditioning Chart B

Age	Masturbation per week total or month (i.e., 2–3x week, 1x month)	Masturbation to fantasy (i.e., 50%)	Masturbation to porn (i.e., 35%)	Masturbation with people as objects (i.e., 10%)	Relational sex (i.e., 5%)
10–15					
15–20					
21–25					
26–30					
31–35					
36–40					
41–45					
46–50					
51–55					
56–60					
61–65					
66+					

In Chart B, put a number "1" by your highest sexually conditioned zone. Place a number "2" by your second highest zone, a "3" by the third and a "4" by the fourth, if any.

At this point it should be obvious to you what kind of sexual brain you have. Look at the chart and think about whether your pattern has changed much over the years. One of my clients said, "Doc, I'm singularly focused on the wrong thing." He realized that he had focused on pornography throughout his whole life, thereby forming an unhealthy sexual pattern. Some of you will be able to see that an unhealthy pattern began early on, but because you stayed sexually faithful to your wife rather than pursuing that pattern, you feel sexually successful and not distracted.

In addition to the sexual conditioning zones, I know that each of my male clients really appreciates seeing how his brain functions. Compare the three images of the brain types we have discussed to understand more clearly where you might locate yourself at the present time.

DIAGRAM 4

Uni-focused

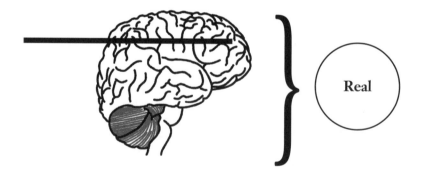

Dual-focused

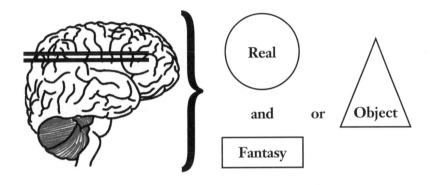

Multi-focused

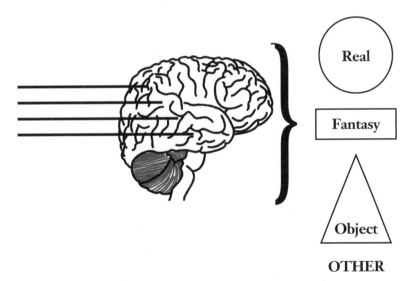

OTHER

Remember that where you see yourself now is not necessarily your finish line. This is true in any area of life. For a couple who is in debt and squandering money, it is possible to become wealthy eventually if they make changes and follow principles required for financial success. I am confident that a victorious journey to sexual success is possible for everyone. Regardless of your sexual conditioning up to now, you *can* achieve successful sexuality.

I know that presently you may be hitting some paradigm turbulence. That's OK! Just keep climbing. As they say here in Colorado, the view will be worth the effort!

TRUE-TO-LIFE STORIES

The following three stories will help you better comprehend the brain types we've discussed. These accounts may also help you further in identifying your own sexual brain type.

~

Charlie has a uni-focused brain. He is forty-six and has been married for twenty-three years. He dated a few girl-friends during high school and college. He also has a Christian background and parents who emphasized sexual purity. They instilled the fear of pregnancy in Charlie after his cousin impregnated a girl and married her at age nineteen.

Charlie experimented some with masturbation, but since he had no access to porn, he never attached to it. Right after college, he married Suzanne, his girlfriend of eighteen months. They first had intercourse on their honeymoon. He has had sex with his wife about two to four times a week over the course of his entire marriage. Charlie looks at his wife with adoration. She's gained a few pounds over the years—and so has he—but he's accepting and loving of her body and brags all the time about how he picked the "right one." To hang around Charlie is, at some point, to be intro-duced to his wife along the way of conversation. Sure, Charlie sees other pretty women regularly at the office where he works, but they are simply coworkers to him. "Suzie," as he calls her, is really what gets his brain think-ing about sex. I know Charlie personally, and he will never be a client in need of sexual help.

~

Martin, who just turned fifty, has led a moderately successful career in a large corporation. He has three children: two boys and a girl who just went off to college a few months ago.

When Martin first came into my office for marriage counseling, he stated that he was "just not happy with his marriage" and sex was routine and boring. His wife, Linda, forty-seven, walks two to four miles a day, is tan, is athletically built and has a smile that could light up Texas. She said they get along OK, but that sex had always been an issue.

Early in the marriage, Linda continued, Martin wanted her to watch pornographic videos with him. She tried it a few times but didn't really like it, and she asked Martin not to do it. Martin regularly asks Linda to participate in something he read about in a pornographic magazine or that he has seen on a pornographic video. She always says no, and he then pouts and sulks for weeks. This is how the marriage goes. Martin says he really loves Linda and the life they've built together. Both want to live the rest of their lives together happily ever after, enjoying their beautiful vacation home overlooking a lake.

When Martin came in for a private therapy session, I asked about his sexual history. He had had access to pornography since he was fourteen years old, when he and a neighborhood kid would steal from the huge porn collection of the boy's dad. He masturbated three to five times a week until he was about thirty years old, and he kept this pattern going a minimum of two times a week for the rest of his marriage. His particular choice in the pornographic magazines was young women with blonde hair and large chests. Linda is an attractive brunette with pretty brown eyes and did not meet any of his preferences.

Martin's sexual past prior to marriage revealed some short-term relationships and one long-term relationship with the girl of his dreams, but she couldn't be faithful to Martin. He also had several one-night stands and three prostitutes who were all blondes.

Martin realized early in our session that he had created acute dual-brain sexuality. When we added it up, almost two-thirds of his sexual releases over the span of his life were with the fantasy blonde and not his athletically built, brunette wife, who has a normal appetite for sex.

Martin responded positively to counsel and began to use many of the principles in this book in his journey toward sexual success. He continues to call me periodically, usually after fishing, to update me happily about the major difference in his life now. He is experiencing a very healthy sex life with Linda and not suffering a duality anymore.

~

This third couple, Roberto and Mary, are clients from quite a while ago. They had been married only eight years when they first came to see me. Roberto and Mary were close to divorcing before they came in for counseling. Yet, Roberto insisted repeatedly that he loved Mary and would do anything to save the marriage.

This is Roberto's second marriage; it is Mary's first. Roberto has two grown children from his first marriage who were raised mostly by his ex-wife. Roberto and Mary have no children of their own.

Roberto is forty-seven and a moderately successful local musician. He plays mostly at bars, in some churches and for an occasional wedding. He has written a few songs and hopes to get them published. Mary is a thirty-six-year-old attractive, successful business manager with a good and steady income.

Roberto's sexual history has included many one-night stands and two short-term affairs, just for the sex. In a private session with me, Roberto said he had had at least twenty-five encounters with different women since being married to Mary. He stated, "I've had sex with anyone available: fat women, women twenty years older than me and younger women of any race or handicap." He added, "If I think I can have sex with a woman at a bar, I do."

Roberto easily identified with the multi-focused brain. He said he had lots of involvement with pornography early in his life and currently had a room full of it at his home. Starting early on, he has been sexual with over three hundred women during his life. He was repeatedly unfaithful to his first wife and can't remember a woman with whom he was ever monogamous. He stated that he was always on the hunt for more, different and better sex. Roberto watched a show about sex addiction on television and identified himself as a sexual addict. When having sex with Mary, over 90 percent of the time he fantasized about other women or pornography he had viewed earlier.

In spite of this sexual history, Roberto was truthful about wanting to save his marriage, and he did. He has been successfully monogamous for quite a while now. How do I know? Mary has him regularly take a polygraph examination regarding his sexuality with other women as well as his viewing of pornography, and she faxes me his results along with a "thank you."

Not only has this couple stayed married, but Roberto has also learned how to enjoy intimacy and three-dimensional sex. He told me he is experiencing the best sex of his life and is blown away by how close he feels to Mary during sex.

∾

These accounts should encourage you to pursue your own journey toward sexual success. Reading this book has become the starting point for your personal journey. By applying the principles laid out here, you are pursuing a path along which you will discover territories of successful sexuality you never knew existed.

THREE

Three Major Battlefronts

W hile counseling men in the area of their sexuality, I have discovered they are often confronted with three major battlefronts. Battlefronts are common sexual issues that can interrupt a man's journey to sexual success and keep him from inheriting the land God promised to him with his gift of sexuality.

As a therapist, literally years of my life have been given to listening to the stories of men who have been affected by one or more of these battlefronts. If one of these sexual issues has derailed your progress toward sexual success, I would encourage you to attack it so that you can reach your desired goals.

Some of the information on the next few pages may not concern you, but for those who are affected by these sexual issues, they are probably affected in a major way. I have experienced two of these three battlefronts myself. I not only am aware of the validity of these distractions, but I also know the way back to the pathway to becoming sexually focused and successful.

For those of you who are not currently affected by these

three battlefronts, I suggest that you read through this chapter anyway. You will be amazed at the understanding you'll gain regarding the behaviors of men you know and to whom you could possibly offer some insight so that they can inherit their "promised land."

BATTLEFRONT 1—ABUSE

When I originally contemplated writing about this battle, I was primarily thinking about sexual abuse. After reflecting over my past clinical experience, however, I realized the need to address two other forms of abuse—physical and emotional—since they can negatively affect a man's sexuality as well.

To be a whole man, your soul must be healed from past pain as much as possible. I was one of those very wounded souls searching for wholeness. I have never met my biological father. My legal father was an alcoholic, which probably means my mother suffered from her own sexual issues. She placed her children in foster homes. I experienced abuse as a teenager as well.

I know what it is to be abused, but I am in no way a whiner. I fervently believe in accepting personal responsibility for the healing of any wounding one has received. This is the way I explain that personal responsibility to my clients. If someone shot me with a bullet, it would not be my fault that I was shot. However, once I have a bullet inside of me, it is my responsibility to get the bullet out and to do any physical therapy necessary to help my body heal. Although I definitely did not create the wound, it is my job to heal from it.

I know people who whine and complain about their past. Not me! My idea of being healed from the effects of a miserable past is to identify your wounds and start cleaning them up so you can become the most fulfilled, life-giving Christian man you can be.

If you did experience sexual, emotional or physical abuse, you probably followed the male code of never telling anyone that it happened. I don't think I talked about any of my trauma until I was in my twenties. If you have experienced trauma, don't worry. I'm not going to suggest therapy at this point. I will, however, give you guidelines for experiencing your healing.

I fervently believe in accepting personal responsibility for the healing of any wounding one has received.

A child can suffer abuse or neglect at the hands of Dad, Mom, strangers, relatives or neighbors. Verbal abuse and shaming can be an ongoing event comprised of a parent or guardian repeatedly attacking the child's soul with verbal assaults.

These painful assaults are like shooting bullets into the soul. In self-protection, the child may choose not to trust others anymore, pulling away in emotional and spiritual isolation from others. The result will most likely be that he won't develop skills for interpersonal relationships. He is walled off from others because he is convinced that "all relationships cause pain." Think of all his future relationships that will become strained because of this abuse: parent-child, employer-employee, teacher-student, husband-wife and so on. He may even conclude, "Why should I fall in love? Why should I fully give myself to any relationship?"

The second way that victims of abuse sometimes choose to respond is to become perfectly wonderful. The goal: to become so smart, handsome, strong or financially successful that nobody would ever suspect that your soul is wounded. After all, when they see how wonderful you are, they can't imagine that you were ever injured or taken advantage of. These people look great on the outside; they often have relationships that look picture-perfect. However, they rarely can connect spiritually or emotionally in an intimate relationship.

Life for these men looks great on the outside—the expensive car, the extravagant house and a beautiful wife. But their wives tell another inside story that sadly reveals a lack of intimacy in their marriage. These wounded men stay mostly in object-type relationships with all people. They generally can talk football and work, but they are incapable of delving into the deep issues of relationships.

As they continue to protect their soul from anticipated pain, over time these men become less and less able to be intimate. Their wounds become the beams that hold up their walls of isolation, and they become less and less emotionally and spiritually engaged in their sexuality.

The less soul that is available in your sex life, the less sexual satisfaction you can experience with your wife. The more soul available during sex, the more sexual satisfaction will result. If these symptoms describe your pain, you can look forward to a later chapter in which I will give you clear guidelines and exercises to heal your soul of its past wounds so that you can engage all of your soul in the bedroom. Then you will begin to have the absolute best sex of your life! Regardless of your past, your future *can* be sexually satisfying and fulfilling. For those of you who have suffered wounds in the past, the process will involve a little more work, but a better sex life is worth it!

BATTLEFRONT 2—ADDICTIONS

Addictions create another major battlefront that affects many men and keeps them from inheriting their land sexually. Even Christian men can suffer addictions. I personally have counseled with pastors, elders, deacons, Sunday school teachers and Bible school professors who have suffered from a variety of addictions.

Addictions can take control in a man's life for many reasons. The addict can be a soul in pain, as we talked about earlier, and find relief or escape in the "medicine" of his choice, which may be sex, work, alcohol, drugs or food. Or he may be a man whose spiritual life is nonexistent and who uses his addiction to fill his void of God. Lastly, a man can become an addict unintentionally because of a neurological imbalance or do it intentionally for the purpose of a neurological reward.

> # Your addictions not only affect your personal life; they have a dramatic effect on your spouse as well.

The man whose brain is chemically depressed or suffers from a disorder such as bipolar disorder may find that sex, work, alcohol, drugs or food increases certain chemicals in his brain that actually make him feel better. Someone who is chemically depressed as a teenager may find that alcohol or masturbation stabilizes him. Continually using these as his "fix" could eventually create an addiction, while at the same time positively helping to balance the depression.

Another type of addiction affects the man whose life revolves around his single neuropathic reward of choice. He may allow himself to get his high through risk or excitement and could get addicted to this particular activity to the point where it excludes real connecting with others.

Addictive behavior usually includes at least three of the following characteristics:

- Spending more time involved in a behavior than the person expected

- Many unsuccessful attempts to reduce time spent on the behavior or to stop the behavior

- A great deal of time required to recover from the behavior

- Social or work plans affected by the behavior

- Choosing to pursue the behavior instead of participating in normal social, occupational or recreational activity

- Choosing to continue the addictive behavior in spite of knowing it has caused problems

- A marked tolerance for the behavior, meaning it takes more to get the same effect

- Withdrawal symptoms if not pursuing the behavior

- Continuing to pursue the behavior to avoid withdrawal symptoms

As you honestly apply to your behavior patterns the above list of addiction characteristics, you may discover that your life is being negatively impacted by addictions of which you were not aware. Of course, your addictions not only affect your personal life; they have a dramatic effect on your spouse as well.

While conducting a study for a book I wrote called *Partners: Healing From His Addiction,* I discovered that women who are in a relationship with a sex addict are much more likely to suffer from depression, lower self-esteem and eating disorders. Observe your wife for a moment. Does she resemble this description? If she does, as an addict you may bear some of the responsibility for her suffering. On the flip side, it's not your spouse who can make you better: It's you.

If you're struggling with an addiction of any kind, it's

necessary first of all to find out why you're addicted. I suggest that you attend a support group. If the addiction is sexual in nature, I strongly recommend my book *The Final Freedom: Pioneering Sexual Addiction Recovery*, which you may have seen discussed on *Oprah*, *Good Morning America* or other national television programs and radio shows, as well as in the print media.

A person who suffers from addictions, for whatever reason, is limiting his ability to achieve sexual success. For the man who strives to recover from his addictions, sex becomes incredibly better than it was when the addictions ruled his life. As we have stated, the more soul that you have to give your wife during intimacy, the better sex you will experience.

BATTLEFRONT 3—SEXUAL ANOREXIA

Most people are not familiar with the term *sexual anorexia*, but it can be a huge player in sexual dissatisfaction. When people think of anorexia they often think of skinny women who won't eat due to anorexia nervosa. But there are other forms of anorexia, including sexual anorexia. This condition basically involves an inability to experience true intimacy.

The sexual anorexic won't connect emotionally, spiritually, relationally or sexually. This form of anorexia only affects the primary relationship, such as a husband-and-wife relationship. If you suffer from this scenario, people who know you may think you're a terrific guy. And if they are unaware of difficulties in your marriage, they will wonder why your wife isn't happy with you.

Friends outside of your primary relationship don't know that when you go home you barely communicate with your wife, that you practically avoid her. Almost anything can and does take your time and attention away from her. They don't know that you don't initiate sex with her and that you don't even desire sex with your wife. They don't know about your secret fantasies, your pornography habit or masturbation patterns that you substitute for the intimate time you could be giving to your wife.

If you suffer from sexual anorexia, though you may look great to the outside world, your wife is starving to connect with you. She can't get you to share yourself or your feelings with her, no matter what she does. Her conversations with you are more like communication between roommates than between a husband and wife.

Sexual anorexia is an active, almost compulsive, withholding of emotional, spiritual and sexual intimacy in a primary relationship. It is a constant sabotaging of any connectedness that should happen, for example, with your wife. The sexual anorexic intentionally will not initiate sharing his heart or his world with his wife. Though this condition is not rampant among men, for those who do struggle with this issue, sexual success will be impossible until it is resolved.

SEXUAL ANOREXIA SELF-TEST

Taking the following short quiz can help you identify sexual anorexia in yourself. Sexual anorexia also has a female form that can keep a couple intimately or sexually stalemated.

Sexual Anorexia Self-Test

Answer yes or no to the following questions relating to the course of your relationship.

1. Would your spouse feel you keep yourself so busy that you have little time for her (not family time, but just time for her alone)?

   Y___ N___

2. Would your spouse feel that if problems arise in the relationship, you are more likely to

focus on them as the problem before owning your side of the problem? Y___ N___

3. Would your spouse feel that you withhold love from her (not sex)? Y___ N___

4. Would your spouse feel that you withhold praise from her? Y___ N___

5. Would your spouse feel that you withhold sex from her or that you withhold yourself spiritually and emotionally during sex with her? Y___ N___

6. Would your spouse feel that you are unwilling or unable to discuss your feelings with her? Y___ N___

7. Would your spouse feel that you have ungrounded or ongoing criticism of her? Y___ N___

8. Would your spouse feel that you use silence or anger as a means of control in the relationship? Y___ N___

9. Would your spouse feel that you control or shame her in financial issues? Y___ N___

If you answered "yes" to five or more questions, sexual anorexia is most likely present in your relationship. Be encouraged that there is hope—sexual anorexia can go into full remission. I have had numerous clients throughout the years who were so sexually anorexic that they had not had sex for over ten years. Often within six to eight weeks of developing their intimacy skills, these clients not only began having the best sex of their lives, but they and their wife actually started liking each other again.

Regardless of where you located your battlefront (sexual trauma, addiction or sexual anorexia), you can become sexually successful. I have counseled men from all walks of life with these issues—some with all three—and have seen their sex lives make an incredible about-face. What follows is a very practical, non-touchy-feely approach to defeating each of these sexual issues. In my counseling practice I have assisted my clients in winning these battles thousands of times. This approach works if you pick up your sword and charge toward the work required to bring you the success you desire.

Some of you reading this chapter may not have any of the battles we have discussed to work through. If you don't, be thankful! You might just want to glance though these approaches to resolving sexual trauma and overcoming addiction and sexual anorexia, however, because this understanding may allow you to help someone struggling with these issues that are so very prevalent in our culture and even in the church today.

RESOLVING SEXUAL TRAUMA

We have described the problems caused by three terrible battlefronts that threaten to defeat many men in their quest for sexual success. If you have identified any of these battlefronts in your life, prepare now to be equipped with the armaments that will help you defeat your enemy.

The first battlefront we described was abuse, which included sexual, physical and emotional trauma. Sexual trauma affects approximately 15 percent of the male population in America. Most occurs at the hands of older men, older boys or male peers. A smaller percentage of victims are sexually traumatized by older women, baby-sitters or relatives. Regardless of the gender of your perpetrator or their age, the following exercise will help you tremendously in overcoming sexual trauma you experienced, and it will give you closure to these past painful events. In case you need more help than these two exercises offer, seek the assistance of a professional counselor who specializes in sexual trauma.

You are honoring God by cleansing your temple to restore it to its divine purpose.

The process I outline is based in an analogy drawn from the scriptural account of Jesus cleansing the temple. As you read this account, take note of how Jesus identified the sin and expressed His anger against it, with the intent of cleansing the temple and restoring it to its God-given purpose (Luke 19:45–48).

The Scriptures use the analogy of a temple in reference to our bodies: "Do you not know that your body is a temple of the Holy Spirit, who is in you, whom you have received from God? You are not your own; you were bought at a price. Therefore honor God with your body" (1 Cor. 6:19–20). As you apply the following principles, realize that you are honoring God by cleansing your temple to restore it to its divine purpose.

As you consider this process of resolving past trauma, it is important for you to realize that when you experienced trauma, your life was negatively impacted. Even if you didn't want it to be, it was. In fact, when someone is being sexual, they are absolutely in the most vulnerable state possible. So if a sexual perpetrator used you as a sex object, that trauma impacted all three dimensions of your being—spirit, soul and body.

Not all, but many traditional therapists are ineffective in handling sexual trauma because they try to deal with this three-dimensional woundedness using a one-dimensional method. The healing process outlined here addresses all three parts of your woundedness.

As we have discussed, sexual trauma is not the only

trauma a Christian man can experience growing up. You may have suffered emotional, physical or even spiritual trauma. The healing process outlined here is effective for all forms of trauma.

Symbolic confrontation

To begin the process of resolving past trauma, follow the instructions below that will enable you symbolically to confront the perpetrator of the trauma you experienced. These steps will initiate your healing and begin to bring needed closure to past traumatic events that have impacted your life.

First, list the offender(s) in your life. List the offenses they committed, your age at the time of the offense and a brief description of the offense.

Example:

- When I was seven years old, a neighbor boy had me . . .

- Dad left me when I was nine.

- A female baby-sitter forced me, at age twelve, to . . .

- A stranger in an adult bookstore did . . .

Rank these offenses in order of intensity, with the number "1" marking the highest level of trauma you feel you experienced.

Second, you will need to confront each perpetrator symbolically, one at a time, using the following format. Before starting, turn the phones off and make sure you have complete privacy for your confrontation.

Confront only one person at a time, beginning with the worst offender. I usually recommend that you allow three days between confronting each perpetrator. All four of these components for symbolic confrontations are very important:

1. Write your anger letter.

2. Warm up for your symbolic confrontation.
3. Read your letter aloud.
4. Carry out your symbolic confrontation (hit the target).

NOTE: As a word of caution, if you have heart trouble or other health issues, consult your physician before beginning these symbolic confrontations.

Carry out these instructions for each offender:

1. *Anger letter.* Write down the name of your offender, if you know it, and then write him or her a letter expressing all your feelings: If you could put this person in a chair, strap them down and gag them, what would you like to say to him or her regarding what they have done to you? Include in your letter the effects his or her actions have had on your life, your relationships and your sexuality. Don't hold back any thoughts or feelings, and don't worry about your language either. More than likely, sexual abuse has dramatically affected your life and kept you from being completely sexually successful. Your perpetrators deserve the rage you feel about them. Write it all in your letter. Do not mail the letter—this is strictly a therapeutic process for your own healing.

2. *Warm up.* You need a racquet or bat (most stores carry sport bats that are padded) along with a mattress, pillow or punching bag. Swinging your bat, strike the mattress with small, medium, large and extra-large hits. Practice doing this a time or two. Also, warm up your voice by saying "no," getting louder with each hit. Although this may seem awkward at first, it is an essential step to your symbolic confrontation, which will enable you to release your rage.

3. *Read your letter aloud.* Now read your letter as if you were talking to your offender. This is an important

part of the process as well. As you read the letter, expect strong feelings to well up inside of you. That is normal. The next step will help discharge those feeling of trauma.

4. *Hit the target.* Go after your perpetrator (the mattress) with your bat. Really let him or her have it. You can hit, yell, kick or whatever you need to do to get the rage, shame and hatred out of you and put it back on your perpetrator where it belongs. It's their shame you have been carrying all these years, not yours.

This last step can take anywhere from ten minutes to an hour depending on the intensity of the ordeal you experienced and how deeply the pain is lodged inside of you. The more emotion you let out, the better you will feel afterward. You are now taking the bullet out of your being—spirit, soul and body—and giving it back to the person responsible for inflicting you with it.

I have personally gone through this symbolic confrontation with each of the offenders in my life. I can look back to a concrete time and place when I pulled their bullets out of my soul and began to heal.

My clients' experiences of healing through these symbolic confrontations vary. Some say they feel better immediately. Others say it takes a few days before they realize that they are free of the bondage that once strangled them. But all say it works for them.

Release through forgiveness

The next step in the process for being healed from trauma after symbolically confronting your perpetrator and addressing your anger is to release yourself from the perpetrator. This release comes through forgiving him or her. It has been said that the benefit of forgiveness is greater for the one who forgives than for the one who is forgiven. My personal and professional experience concurs; forgiving your perpetrator after cleansing your temple of trauma is powerfully therapeutic.

For this exercise you will need two chairs and privacy. Again, turn off the phones and make sure everyone is out of the house. Place the two chairs in the room so that they face each other. Then proceed through the three phases of this exercise:

Phase 1: Sit in one of the chairs. We will call this Chair A for our discussion. From here you will role-play the perpetrator. You can use your perpetrator's name if you know it. If he or she was a stranger, you can give them a name or simply say, "I am the one who abused you."

Acting as the perpetrator in Chair A—let's use "Fred" as an example—face Chair B and imagine yourself sitting in Chair B. As Fred, you can own the abuse, apologize and ask for forgiveness. Be sure to acknowledge the costs to yourself, the victim. Be specific; don't just say, "I'm sorry." Instead, if Fred was an adult who forced you into oral sex as a child, you may say something like, "I am the one who made you perform oral sex. I used you like other boys I had victimized. You were just an object to me when I did this to you. I know I must have damaged your life. I hope you can heal, and I now ask you to forgive me."

Phase 2: After the perpetrator has appropriately apologized to you, then physically get up and move to Chair B. Sitting in Chair B, role-play yourself as receiving this information from your perpetrator. You have just heard him apologize and ask forgiveness for the acts he did toward you and the effect they have had on you.

In Chair B, you can respond any way that you like. You may not be ready to release him or her or forgive at this time. Whatever your thoughts or feelings are, verbalize them aloud to the perpetrator. The purpose of this exercise is for you to be honest. Releasing your perpetrator at some point is a gift you can give to yourself. Their life moved on whether you "let them off the hook" or not. By forgiving and releasing them, you are *not* approving what they did to you. You are simply releasing that behavior from having an influence in your life any longer.

If you are unable to forgive or release your offender at this time, try this exercise again in a month or so. However, if you were able to let go, move on to Phase 3.

Phase 3: Physically move back to Chair A and resume the role of the perpetrator again. Now you need to respond to the forgiveness or the releasing that has been extended toward you. In this case, Fred our perpetrator may say "Thank you for forgiving me. I hope you can move on. Thanks again."

This concludes the process of your symbolic confrontation. This exercise is very powerful for most men. As you complete it you can fully say good-bye to that painful chapter of your life. From this point on the majority of men can view the trauma they experienced as part of their history without any ongoing negative effects in their life. This liberating reality is similar to bearing a scar from an injury but no longer suffering the pain of it.

I hope that all who need to heal from the issue of sexual trauma will complete these exercises. They have changed thousands of men's and women's lives. You can also apply them to traumatic events from your past that aren't sexual in nature. The verbal abuse or physical abuse of a parent may also warrant going through this process.

OVERCOMING ADDICTION

In this section, I will cover only the basic requirements for overcoming addiction. For a more complete understanding of the area of sexual addiction and recovery, I recommend you read and work through the following books:

- Douglas Weiss, *The Final Freedom: Pioneering Sexual Addiction Recovery* (Colorado Springs, CO: Discovery Press, 1998).

- Douglas Weiss, *101 Freedom Exercises: A Christian Guide for Sexual Addiction Recovery*, second edition (Colorado Springs, CO: Discovery Press, 2000).

- Douglas Weiss, *Steps to Freedom: A 12-Step Christian Guide for Sexual Addiction Recovery*, second edition (Colorado Springs, CO: Discovery Press, 2000).

Sexual addiction is by far the leading addiction in the church today. These books will help you gain a better understanding of an addiction and give you many practical tools for your personal recovery as well as the help you need to offer others in your church.

The first step to recovering from your addiction is to acknowledge that you are an addict. No one can help an addict who lives in denial of his problem and thinks that all guys do this or that. To recover, you will have to stop lying to yourself.

Remember that our Father in heaven sees all and knows all. He knows your every thought. He knows if you struggle in this area. He also has heard every prayer you have prayed to stop your secret behavior. He wants you to be free more than you do. You will have Him with you as you fight this battle.

You can recognize your need to heal from a sexual addiction if you find yourself:

- Convinced your behavior has to be secret.

- Continually needing more and more of this behavior to be satisfied.

- Constantly trying and failing to stop a certain behavior.

- Continuing this behavior, knowing your wife doesn't agree and that it is affecting your relationship with her.

Addictions, by definition, will not allow you to recover from them without help. I'm sure you believe that you can handle this yourself. That is the surest way to fail. Again, stop lying to yourself. You are going to need some help to get better. Another man is going to need to be in your life for support.

I see so many Christian men who are trapped by an addiction try to fix it themselves. They have memorized 1 John 1:9:

> If we confess our sins, he is faithful and just and will forgive us our sins and purify us from all unrighteousness.

The problem is that this verse promises forgiveness, not healing. To address your need for healing from sexual addiction, you need to turn back a few pages in your Bible to James 5:16.

> Therefore confess your sins to each other and pray for each other so that you may be healed. The prayer of a righteous man is powerful and effective.

As we mentioned in our discussion of how to overcome lust, a powerful biblical tool for healing is accountability. If you want healing from addiction, you need to be willing to humble yourself to another man and begin to confess the truth of your sin. Scripture declares that as you do so and pray for each other, you will be healed. The apostle James also warns us that:

> God opposes the proud but gives grace to the humble.
> —JAMES 4:6

I don't like this warning much either, but until I accepted it and was willing to humble myself to another man, I was trapped in my behavior patterns. When I started becoming accountable to another person, I began to get free.

Support groups are available to assist men in overcoming all addictions, including sexual addictions. Maybe your excuse for not attending a support group is that you are rich, famous or hold a prominent position in your community, and you're concerned that you will be recognized. I have counseled with men all over the country for many years, and I have never found one instance where the trust of anonymity had been broken. These support groups are a safe place for you to begin to heal.

These men know what you're struggling with and have heard it all. To find a local support group in your area, you can visit our website at www.sexaddict.com or call my office for the closest Freedom Group in your area. A Freedom Group is a Christ-based twelve-step support group for sexual addictions. If your church doesn't have one in place, there are other secular and Christian twelve-step groups for this and other types of addiction.

I encourage churches to establish these much-needed support groups. Our experience is that once a church offers help for the sexually addicted, these groups multiply quickly because of men who are getting healed. You can get free from sexual addiction and become sexually successful.

But don't try to do it all by yourself; it just won't work.

OVERCOMING SEXUAL ANOREXIA

Sexual anorexia and sexual addiction are not mutually exclusive; they sometimes can affect a man simultaneously. If this is true for you, you will need to work through recovery guidelines for sexual addiction and the intimacy exercises for sexual anorexia.

Without daily intimacy with your wife, sexual anorexia can't heal. In a later chapter, I discuss the three daily exercises needed to develop and maintain intimacy with your spouse. For the sexual anorexic, these exercises are essential to his healing. Also, if you rely on your wife to initiate sex, or if you are withholding sex from her, to be healed you will need to establish and adhere to the guidelines given in the chapter about sexual agreement.

Anorexics often purposely sabotage their sex life with their spouse to avoid the threat of intimacy. If you are anorexic, I encourage you to visit our website at www.intimatematters.com and get the ninety-minute video "Sexual Anorexia." After viewing this video, you and your wife will be able to understand this issue and apply the practical solutions offered.

Regardless of the distractions from your past that have plagued you and your spouse, you can now heal and move forward to sexual success. If this process involves a lot of work, start on it immediately. Make your action plan. Mark it in your daily planner or Palm Pilot to make your road to healing a top priority. This will make sexual success much easier to attain. Remember, the more soul you bring into the bedroom, the better it will be for you. Stay focused on your recovery work, and give yourself the gift of sexual success.

FOUR

Shame on Me

Sexual shame poses an enormous obstacle to your sexual success. Harboring shame of any kind can limit your ability to be fully available in the bedroom. This is true even more so when it comes to sexual shame. Since most men keep such shame a secret, the shame often becomes so deeply imbedded that it's almost a part of the man himself.

It's quite obvious when a man has issues with sexual shame. He walks with his head down, doesn't achieve his potential and rarely looks anyone in the eye. Some men may have the appearance of being confident and successful, yet no one really knows them. Why? Because they live out the core belief, "If you really knew me, you wouldn't love or accept me."

Men are sexual beings, and when a man is sexually violated, this vulnerable component of his very existence is abused. As a result, many men carrying sexual shame believe not only that someone has done something bad to them, or they themselves have done something bad, but rather that they *are* bad. Their core belief says they are truly different from other men.

In their minds, the difference is that they *are* bad, wrong and less than others. They feel that they don't measure up to others. These feelings of worthlessness can keep them isolated, walled off and trapped in underachievement.

Since a man is sexual daily, because sexuality is part of him, he will feel this shame daily. It plagues his quiet moments and frightens him in the face of real intimacy. It talks to him when he is alone. He may hear "voices" of:

- "You're no good. If they knew what happened to you sexually, they wouldn't even want to be in the same room with you."

- "You're different."

- "You're weak."

- "You're inadequate."

You can understand that a man with these negative thought patterns repeating in his head could not possibly live sexually unashamed, free or confident. Such sexual disgrace connects to the very core of the masculine soul. In this chapter we will discuss three types of sexual shame. Then I will outline a plan for you to move beyond shame and into sexual acceptance and sexual health.

SEXUAL PERFORMANCE SHAME

This type of sexual shame tries to torment men of all ages. Often a man with this issue feels as if he is not a good lover for such performance reasons as not being able to get or maintain an erection. Overwhelming feelings of disappointment, hurt or rage often follow this experience.

Sexual performance shame is very difficult for a man to live with. The isolation this man feels is incredible. He often feels as if he can't talk to his friends, pastor or doctor. He is so ashamed sexually that he barely feels like a man.

A second issue that triggers this shame among men is

that of premature ejaculation, meaning a man may ejaculate so quickly that the sex act is over in a couple of minutes. This may happen for several reasons; however, the feeling afterwards is still the same—that of inadequacy.

A third issue that causes sexual performance shame is that of not bringing your spouse to orgasm. Some men attach much of their sexual identity to bringing her to orgasm. They often don't realize that not all women are orgasmic in the same manner, and some are only orgasmic by a specific form of manipulation. Some men take this personally and feel sexually inadequate when they experience orgasm but discover their wife needs a different form of stimulation. Over a period of time this can reduce a sexually confident man into a sexually shamed man.

Sexual shame poses an enormous obstacle to your sexual success.

The last issue of sexual performance shame does not have as much to do with the performance as it does with men's anatomy. Some men feel sexual shame solely because of the size of their sex organ. Perhaps they were teased in gym classes as a teenager, or perhaps they compared themselves to others while viewing pornography.

A man suffering this shame rarely shares it with others, but instead he allows that shame to get embedded deep in his heart. What's more, this man experiences shame even though his wife is sexually fulfilled and has verbally and behaviorally demonstrated that she is satisfied. He continues to feel like less of a man than others and rarely internalizes genuine sexual affirmation or praise from his wife; instead he remains muddled in sexual shame. Some men have tried enlargement gadgets and even surgery because they could not accept the way their bodies were made. Often this shame keeps a man from the sexual inheritance he desires.

SEXUAL HISTORY SHAME

Every man has a sexual history. The history of some men only involves their wife. Others have had multiple sexual experiences prior to marriage. As we have discussed earlier, some of these men have also experienced sexual trauma during their sexual history.

Whatever the history, many have sexual memories that bring tremendous shame when recalled. One man told me that when he was younger he worked in a convenience store where a woman continuously called him and talked sexually inappropriately to him. This went on for weeks. One day she invited him to her house. She kept her house totally dark, and they had sex. It was then that he realized she was incredibly obese and significantly older than he was. He had several more sexual encounters with her on various occasions. This man carried tremendous shame as a result of these sexual episodes.

Everyone is different when it comes to sexual shame. What may cause sexual shame for one person to the point that it hinders his future sexual success may not cause another man shame at all. We are all unique when it comes to sexuality, so we experience sexual shame in very different ways as well.

Countless hours of my practice have been spent helping men get and stay free from such disgrace. For some men this shame is tied to an early event in their childhood. For others it stems from a behavior displayed in their adolescence, where they may have cheated on a girlfriend or she cheated on him, and he was ashamed about it. During adolescence numerous men try to experiment sexually, and sometimes these experiments backfire.

A rather common experiment is the solicitation of a prostitute. I've heard repeatedly how cold, empty and cheap the experience felt. Some prostitutes mocked the young men, and the women's words are still stuck in the memories of these men thirty years later.

Some men are ashamed of homosexual behavior from their past. A common event that is hard to let go of occurs when a teenager first goes to an adult bookstore to view a porn flick and, not being aware that leaving the door unlocked is basically a homosexual invitation, the teen is accosted by a man. I have heard hundreds of stories of this happening. The boy definitely wasn't ready for the encounter, but since all sex feels good at the time, he participated. Now, twenty years later, he still wonders whether he is a homosexual. Additionally, as the teen matures, he may easily fall into using women as objects and totally disregarding them as people. Several men with this type of background have all but raped the women they dated. Others have committed date rape or have been involved in gang rapes.

Another cause of shame from your past could include sexual behavior with yourself during adolescence or young adulthood. Many feel guilty about their masturbation habits. This guilt can arise from the behavior itself, the frequency of the masturbation or from the type of porn that was viewed while masturbating. Also, incredible shame can be linked to objects used or clothing worn during self-sex.

A sexual secret in some men's sexual history involves abortions. They have impregnated a girlfriend who is then forced to abort their baby. In other cases, the man contracted or spread sexually transmitted diseases. Some men have visible marks left on their bodies from these diseases. While the treatment can bring quick relief, the memories are lifelong. Contracting an STD is excruciatingly shameful and is an unforgettable part of one's sexual history.

Scores of men went through a relatively positive and sexually healthy adolescence. But the issue of sexual shame doesn't always stem from one's youth; adult men can get involved in sexual behaviors that cause shame as well. Adultery is one example. I have heard at least a thousand men tell me not only their regret and guilt over their affairs, but also the deep, almost unbearable shame they still feel. Remember that such shame grows from two roots: the immoral behavior and the belief that they themselves are bad.

I have heard men from the ages of twenty to seventy tell their stories of adultery. Men with any number of spiritual backgrounds—pastors, missionaries, deacons, youth workers in the church—have shared with me the great shame they carry because of their sex acts outside of their marriages. These men come from varied financial backgrounds, from those who are poor college students to some who are among the wealthiest men in our nation. This shame appears to run deeper and affect men's sexual success more than any other behavior in their sexual history. The shame is rarely disclosed unless the man gets caught or decides to come clean about it.

Men caught in these situations need to get honest with themselves, though that can be very difficult. I have seen many strong men cry so hard that they were on the floor instead of in the chair when their secret came out. Their pain and anguish have totally convinced me that though adultery may be attractive in the moment of temptation, its end is sheer bitterness.

From the above discussion we can conclude that shame in your sexual history can strike during any part of your sexual development. Sexual shame is unique to your sexual personality and beliefs, and only you know if you have it in your life. If you are concealing sexual shame—and most men are—later in this chapter I will walk you through some ways to close the door for good to that shameful episode of your life.

I am aware of the limitations that sexual shame can bring into the bedroom. I also know what it is like to have no sexual shame at all and what *that* can bring to the bedroom. You may have heard the old saying, "I've been poor, and now I'm rich. Rich is better." The same applies here: "I have had sexual shame, and I have been without sexual shame. Life without sexual shame is much better."

SEXUAL DEVIANCY SHAME

While sexual deviancy is rarely addressed in male sexuality books, it is a powerful cause of shame. Sexual deviancy and the shame that is attached to it can be the result of one of two things: a sex act that you believe is deviant or acts that actually are deviant and considered illegal.

When I refer to acts of sexual deviancy in this book, I am referring to the second category, or illegal sexual behaviors. These behaviors include voyeurism, exposing yourself in public, rape, encouraging a woman to drink alcohol so that she makes a sexual choice in your favor, sexually touching or viewing others without their consent, or any sex acts with a minor or a child.

These sexually deviant behaviors are not prevalent among the majority of the male population. For some men it may have comprised a one-time event, perhaps as a young person. For others sexual deviancy may involve more frequent behavior. The shame caused by these behaviors keeps many men from any possibility of being sexually successful. The man acting out these behaviors can't be honest about his sexuality for fear of imprisonment. The shame is usually attached to the actual sex act as well as to the man's thoughts that he must be a horrible person to even think such deviant behaviors are enjoyable.

Often behaviors that a man once thought of as sexually deviant become acceptable to him over time because he becomes desensitized through exposure to pornography, masturbation or fantasies. Now he attaches sexual pleasure to what he once considered abnormal. Other men may not enjoy the behavior, but because of their experimentation, they now consider themselves sexually deviant.

This last area of sexual deviant shame can come to some

men just by the sheer exposure to deviancy. Some men may cruise porn sites on the Internet, and a screen pops up about something they would normally consider deviant, but it sexually arouses them. They now may believe they are bad because what they considered as bad behavior has sexually aroused them.

I have spent many hours with men who have never engaged in a sexually deviant behavior and yet they have sexual deviancy shame because they viewed this type of pornography or read stories of this behavior and got aroused. Remember, shame wears many different faces.

Sexual shame can come from all kinds of avenues, and men handle shame differently. One man may experience this shame and become an isolated, insecure under-achiever. At the other extreme is a man with this shame who becomes the highly successful overachiever. Yet he too remains isolated and disconnected. Between these two extremes, there are also various ways men handle sexual shame.

Having described the problems of sexual shame, we are now ready to offer practical solutions to resolving this shame. We will list specific solutions for your problem behaviors. You may want to read all the solutions or look for the solution for your problem area. To summarize, the areas of sexual shame that we have discussed so far are:

- Sexual performance shame

- Sexual history shame

- Sexual deviancy shame

Solutions to these areas of shame will follow in the same order listed above. Over the years I have counseled many men through each of the types of shame listed. Regardless of your past, you can move forward and achieve your sex-ual inheritance.

SOLUTIONS TO SEXUAL PERFORMANCE SHAME

ADMIT YOUR PROBLEM.

The first step in dealing with any form of shame is acknowledging that it is a part of your life. Write out the specific sexual shame with which you have struggled. Your statements might look something like:

- I feel sexual shame about not being able to get or maintain an erection with my wife for _____ percent of the time. This has been going on for _____ number of years.

- I feel sexual shame about not being able to bring my wife to an orgasm. This happens _____ percent of the time and has been going on for _____ years.

- I feel sexual shame about the size of my sexual organ. I first remember feeling such shame when I was _____ years old. I feel this shame mostly when _____.

For some men, just reading the above statements can bring up feelings of shame. But the first stage of the solution is to write down the types of shame you're facing.

Next, to help you articulate your problem, write out your feelings about these issues. In Appendix B, there is a Feelings List you can utilize to get you started. Here's an example of how to sort out your feelings:

I have sexual shame about ejaculating so quickly while having sex with my wife. This behavior occurs 20 percent of the time we are sexual together. This has been going on for the past three years. The feeling I have about this issue is *self-doubt* that I am ever going to get over this. I also feel *embarrassed, unmanly, ashamed* and *degraded* whenever it happens. I feel *weak* and *less than* other men shortly afterward. I feel *stuck* when I try to talk to my wife about this. I feel *out of control* and *doubtful* of my wife's love toward me. I feel *alone* because I haven't talked to a doctor about this. I feel *afraid* because I don't know if something is really physically wrong. I also feel *secretive* because I do have some sexual secrets and masturbate more than I let my wife know.

Writing down your feelings is vital to freeing yourself from the heavy weight of shame that has oppressed you. Without completing this step, you may stay emotionally stuck in this issue, which in turn will keep you from making an action plan for your own sexual success.

A final aspect of acknowledging your problem involves processing the shame. To do this, write down your fears or concerns about this issue. The following example may be helpful.

My fears are that if I acknowledge my problem:

- It's only going to get worse.

- My wife will love me less.

- I will think more about it, which will make it worse.

- If I go to the doctor, I am afraid he will tell me something is wrong with me.

- I am afraid I will hate myself.

Fears don't have to be logical, rational or even realistic. Fear is a feeling, and it doesn't need reality to exist. Admitting to the fear is the first and most essential part of loosening its grip and ridding yourself of it. Only then can you begin to think rational thoughts that will factually dismiss these fears. Then you can objectively concede that the fears aren't true, your wife really does love you and so forth. After you have followed the above guidelines to help you to acknowledge your problem, you are ready to experience personal freedom from it by forgiving yourself.

Fear is a feeling, and it doesn't need reality to exist.

FORGIVE YOURSELF.

One of the most difficult steps in dealing with this issue of sexual shame may be asking forgiveness from yourself. This might sound peculiarly trite, but I have found that if men can own their behavior and forgive themselves for it, they are much more likely to move into the next few steps that will rid themselves of the sexual shame. You can process this forgiveness in the same practical way that you earlier processed your symbolic confrontation issues.

Place two chairs facing each other. Sit in one chair (Chair A) and symbolically imagine yourself in the other chair (Chair B). Talk to the self in Chair B and ask forgiveness for whatever the performance issue is. Then move to Chair B and respond to yourself (hopefully forgiving yourself). Go back to Chair A and respond to being forgiven. Let me give you an example.

In our example, Bob is sitting in Chair A. The symbolic "Bob" in Chair B will be "Bob 2." Bob's issue is premature ejaculation. An example of Bob's discussion might go something like this:

> **Bob:** Bob 2, I want to ask you to forgive me for carrying the shame all this time about ejaculating so quickly. I know it's affecting you, and the fear I have caused in your life becomes incredible at times. It has put a wedge in your life between you and your wife. I'm sorry, and I ask you to forgive me for making you ashamed of yourself, even to the point where you won't talk about it to anyone.

(Bob moves to Chair B and now role-plays himself as Bob 2.)

Bob 2: Bob, thank you for finally talking about this. It's not the end of the world. Hey, you have been a great lover to your wife for twenty-three years. You're getting older, and you haven't even gotten a doctor's opinion yet. I forgive you for dragging your feet about this and isolating this topic from your wife, Jan. I really want to move forward on this. This shame is worse than the actual problem. I forgive you. Now let's get to the bottom of this. You're a great guy, a great husband and a great dad. Let's move on!

(Bob moves to Chair A again and responds to what Bob 2 told him.)

Bob: Thanks, Bob 2, for forgiving me. That was probably the hardest thing I have done in a long time. Thanks for encouraging me and being on my side. I think you're right; I can now move forward. I'm glad we are on the same team.

This exercise is one that I have my clients do in my office. It has been a powerful tool to release them from sexual shame. I strongly encourage anyone with sexual shame to set up two chairs and just do the exercise. Don't try to decide if it will work or not; don't try to process through it until after you have done the exercise. It can really help start flushing out the sexual performance shame issues so that you can be much more sexually successful.

Overcoming the grief

Forgiving yourself is a big step, but it's not the last step necessary to getting rid of sexual shame. Another vital process involves acceptance. When big emotional issues impact your life, you often experience one of six different stages of grief. To help you identify where you may be in processing your grief, here are brief descriptions of each stage of grief:

Shock: A numb feeling when you don't know what to do or how to feel with the information you have received.

Denial: You feel that what you're dealing with can happen to anybody. It's not really a problem. You are denying the reality of that which is causing you shame.

Anger: You are feeling mad that this is happening. You may be angry because of the way you are built, or that you ejaculate quickly, or that you can't bring your spouse to orgasm.

Bargaining: You may begin to feel there is something you can do to compensate and make things better. If your first line of reasoning doesn't work, you will often try something else. Or you may believe the solution rests with someone other than yourself. ("The problem will get better if only my wife would lose weight.") Basically, you are emphasizing one variable, trying to change it, so as to avoid the painful reality and ignore its existence.

Sadness: You recognize that the painful reality does exist, and you are sad about it.

Acceptance: The painful reality exists, and it is now a part of your life. You can reasonably expect a certain outcome. You finally accept this and can begin productively living your life with this issue. You now believe that you consist of much more than just this issue, and you can make the best of it.

Acceptance has been described as the end of grief, but it can be a difficult place to reach for some men who grieve over a particular sexual issue. Accepting reality is a tremendous achievement. Let's take Bob for example. After his plan of action was in place, he realized that his issue might continue to occur 20 percent of the time. Bob went to his doctor with his problem, and his doctor told him that since he is eighty-seven years old and is still able to be sexually successful 80 percent of the time, he's doing great!

When Bob accepts that he's normal for an eighty-seven-year-old, he accepts reality and will be able to accept himself more easily. Bob also realizes if he brings his eighty-four-year-old wife to orgasm in a way other than what he is accustomed to, he will still feel like a sexual success.

SOLUTIONS TO SEXUAL HISTORY SHAME

For those of you who have shame attached to your sexual history, I will provide an outline of proactive things you can do to move toward sexual success. I warn you that some of the exercises may be uncomfortable for you, but sexual success is right ahead of you.

BE SPECIFIC.

Sexual history shame is attached to a specific event. You may have had sex with a prostitute or a woman you didn't like; you may have date-raped, gotten a woman drunk so that you could take advantage of her or had an unwanted homosexual encounter. Whatever your situation, you need to be as specific as possible during this exercise.

Write down your entire sexual history. Write how old you were when the event happened, how old the perpetrator was, the type of sexual encounter and whether the event caused you shame. This will enable you to see any recurring types of shame.

Next, tell someone what happened. I want you to tell your deepest, darkest, most ugly secrets to another person. I realize this may be outright frightening, but if you don't confide in someone, your soul will remain sick. You must deal with your shame head-on.

Here are some points to note when choosing someone in whom to confide:

- A professional psychologist or marriage counselor is my first recommendation. You can trust them to not tell a soul about what you have done since it is illegal for them to do so, except in the case of illegal behavior. (For more on this topic, see Solutions for Sexual Deviancy Shame below.) While female therapists are great, I strongly suggest seeing a male therapist because your shame is connected to your male sexuality.

- Others you can trust to keep a confidence are a professional member of a spiritual community, such as a pastor or other spiritual mentor.

- If you choose to confide in a friend, you do run the risk of being exposed in the future. Remember, those who love you today may feel differently tomorrow.

APOLOGIZE.

Some men have gone back to the women to whom they caused pain and apologized. However, if you're married or in a committed relationship, such action should be a joint decision. I don't recommend doing this with an ex-lover. I do recommend this step if the person you have hurt is your present wife. You can then own—take responsibility for—the past pain you have caused her and move forward together.

In the case of ex-lovers, making *symbolic* amends with two chairs works amazingly well. Here's an example of how David handled this with a situation involving his old girlfriend named Sue.

> **David in Chair A:** Sue, I really need to apologize and ask for your forgiveness. When we dated I lied to you countless times. I slept with other women, including your best friend Connie. I not only hurt you, but I

ruined a lifelong friendship that you had. I need you to forgive me for these behaviors.

(David physically gets up and sits in Chair B. He now assumes the role of Sue.)

David as Sue in Chair B: Well, David, you really were a liar, and I spent many a night confused, crying or hating you. I didn't understand your problems, but that was ten years ago. Now I have a great husband and two kids, and I live where I have always dreamed of living. I feel sorry for you and your choices. I can forgive you and accept your apology. I hope you have moved on with your life and have become a decent human being.

(David moves back to Chair A and responds to Sue's extension of forgiveness.)

David in Chair A: Thank you, Sue. You always were a good person. Thank you for forgiving me. I am glad life has turned out well for you.

Continue to go through your sexual history in this manner, and check off the names of those whom you know you have hurt as you apologize to each. This symbolic apology really works to rid yourself of the shame you have accumulated over the years because of wronging others.

I have found that men with painful sexual shame do best when they also ask themselves for forgiveness. You have let yourself down, and you now need to forgive yourself. You can also alleviate shame by doing a forgiveness exercise symbolically with Jesus.

SOLUTIONS TO SEXUAL DEVIANCY SHAME

Men suffering from sexual deviancy shame should follow the same steps as those outlined under sexual history shame with one caution: You need to know that if your behavior was illegal and you confide in a clergyman or a paid psychologist, therapist or psychiatrist, they are bound by the law to report your information to the legal authorities. Statutes of limitations do apply, so you may want to familiarize yourself with the law beforehand.

Regardless of how you have acquired sexual shame, that shame has caused a roadblock to the sexual success you are capable of. I urge you to take the directions in this chapter seriously. I have assisted many men working through their sexual shame and have seen them reclaim their freedom and sexuality.

Sexuality without shame is probably one of the greatest feelings in the world. Each man reading this book deserves to work toward that feeling. I hope you do what's necessary for your sexual inheritance.

ACTION POINTS TO BLAST SEXUAL SHAME

We have discussed specific solutions for three different types of shame. The following action points apply to all three areas of shame we have described. Understanding their importance to your journey toward sexual success will help you make the right choices regardless of the source of your shame.

TALK.

Secrecy is the strength of shame. This is true regardless of the source or the type of shame you suffer. Research has consistently supported the fact that something beneficial happens when you talk about your secrets. While you may be "as sick as your secrets," as the adage goes, it is still true that "confession is good for the soul."

For many men, this is the most difficult part. You always want to look good, feel smart and be successful and strong. Unfortunately, God doesn't make perfect people, so at times we are not so good, not so smart, not so successful and not so strong. When it comes to sexuality these feelings of wanting always to be perfect can be even greater.

Sharing your secrets is essential to moving past your shame into claiming your sexual inheritance. When you decide to take the leap, the first question that comes mind is, "With whom can I talk?" Here are some suggestions:

- A trained professional counselor/psychologist or sex therapist

- A pastor whom you trust

- A doctor to rule out any physiological problem

- A male friend you know who has had similar issues

- Your wife, a friend who loves you and whom you can trust

In order to muster up the courage to discuss your problems, it may be helpful to practice by symbolically placing the person you want to talk to in a chair and talking to him or her. Whether or not you conduct a practice rehearsal, start talking! This alone can help separate the shameful feelings you have from the real issue at hand.

Be proactive.

If you're having a problem with a performance issue, there are several action plans to help:

- ❏ Go to a doctor.

- ❏ Read a book that addresses your particular performance issue. Practice the recommended techniques that are acceptable to you.

- ❏ Take medication if it's recommended.

- ❏ Visit a sex therapist.

- ❏ See a professional counselor, psychologist or addiction counselor.

- ❏ If you are experiencing depression and you think this is part of the issue, make an appointment with a psychiatrist.

- ❏ Regularly practice with your wife the techniques your counselor recommends.

- ❏ If your wife is not orgasmic, go to the doctor with her.

As you go through this process, determine to accept reasonable outcomes based on your factual information, such as your age, your health and so forth. Part of life is accepting what is handed to you. If you have done the best you can on your action points, it will be easier for you to accept your situation.

Honor yourself.

When God created mankind, He included a wonderful commentary of their sexual nature. In Genesis 2:25 we read, "And they were both naked, the man and his wife, and were not ashamed" (NKJV). God never intended your sexuality to cause a sense of shame.

One of the best things you can do for yourself in regards to eliminating shame is simply not do things that you know you'll become ashamed of. If you make a lifestyle of doing the right things, you're more likely to build a positive self-esteem. Also, if you do good for others without letting them know about it, you will feel even better about yourself.

Imagine if all the secrets you had inside of you consisted only of how you had helped others! Life without shame is much more satisfying, incredibly so. If you do commit a less-than-wonderful act, talk about it as soon as possible so shame can't grow. I hope you will honestly evaluate your sexual shame so you can be freed and claim your sexual success.

FIVE

The M Word

By far, one of the most controversial subjects in the church today regarding male sexuality is masturbation. As the church reflects the more sexually open society, men are openly discussing this subject more. In our Western culture this issue can be divisive in some circles of Christianity, depending on if you are more liberal or conservative in your view of what you believe about masturbation.

To make matters worse, few, if any, church denominations have a written doctrinal stance on masturbation. Combining this lack of attention in the church to the issue with the fact that men get little to no information from their fathers about sexuality has resulted in great misunderstanding and emotionally based reactions about masturbation.

On our journey toward sexual success, we understand that in some places the climb is going to be rocky. This issue of masturbation is one of those rocky places. But if you will stay with the climb, I guarantee that you will learn more about masturbation in the following pages and that you will be able to conclude intelligently for yourself and for your son(s) where you stand on this important male sexual issue.

THREE TYPES OF MASTURBATION

Men generally fall into three categories of experience when it comes to masturbation. As you read through this section, you probably will quickly identify with the category that describes your experience. That's the easy part. The hard part will be to believe that the other two categories even exist for other men who identify their experience with them.

The reason men often believe that their category of masturbation is the only reality that exists is that most men base their thought processes on their own experiential template. Our own experiences often limit our thinking process. To put it another way, I think that what I experience is the way it is.

For example, I have had bad experiences trying to fix things around the house. I was never taught how to be a handyman by any of my fathers. For this reason, my experience tells me that all men, except professionals, are bad at handyman work. In conversations with my peers about not being Mr. Fix-it, my thinking is validated by their experience—they also call professionals to fix things around the house.

In order to believe that an average guy can fix most things in his house with no problem, I have to think outside of my experience. Of course, there are guys like that. I see them at Home Depot all the time. But if I limit my thinking only to my experience, I find it hard to believe.

I hope this example of thinking based on experience will help us in our discussion of the issue of masturbation. As I walk through the three masturbation types, please be patient. In the categories that do not apply to your experience, trust that I know for a fact there are men to whom they do apply.

MASTURBATION TYPE A

Of the three types of masturbation, Type A is by far the smallest camp in the Western world and the hardest for those who are not in it to believe that it actually exists. The man who is Type A has never masturbated in his entire life. Some of you are thinking, *No way!* Remember that just because it's not your experience doesn't mean it doesn't exist.

During my travels, as I lecture at men's conferences across the country, I often ask the men to categorize their type of masturbation. I have met only fourteen men over the years that fit into Type A, and three of them go to my church! According to them, masturbation didn't make sense, or they just didn't think to do it.

I was surprised to learn that in some nations masturbation is not the norm. A minister from another nation, whom I know and trust, told me that most men in his country do not masturbate. When I asked why this was not a part of the culture, he told me that in his country masturbation was thought to be a sign of weakness. Can you imagine a whole country of men not masturbating? I think most of my readers would find that difficult to comprehend. Even in our culture, though such men may be extremely in the minority, believe me, that they are out there.

MASTURBATION TYPE B

In the Type B pattern of masturbation, the man's decision for his behavior has been made usually between the ages of twelve and sixteen. When this teenager begins to masturbate, he stays fully "connected" to himself during the act, i.e., he does not lust or create sexual fantasies with girls he knows. And he would never use pornography during masturbation. For this boy, the masturbation experience is simply engaging in a bodily function.

This teenager generally doesn't struggle with lust. Since he doesn't fantasize, he doesn't feel the guilt or shame often involved with masturbation. He feels no separation from God and goes on with the rest of his day as if nothing happened. He does not live in a fantasy sexual world, and he doesn't use masturbation to meet the emotional needs in his life. He just stays connected, releases and moves on.

Again, some of you are scratching your head saying, "No way! How could someone even do that without visual stimulus?" Remember that just because this is not your experience doesn't negate the fact that it still is possible for others.

Remember our earlier conversation about the brain and sex? The young man in this Type B category does not connect in his brain to anything. Often when this man gets married, his masturbation behavior disappears or becomes very infrequent.

MASTURBATION TYPE C

Masturbation Type C represents the disconnected camp where objects are used during masturbation, whether it is a fantasy or an actual physical item. Teenage boys in this camp use fantasy, pornography or some form of objectifying women not only to arouse them during masturbation, but also to bring them to a point of ejaculation. For this teen to enter the world of fantasy, pornography and objectification, he has to spiritually and emotionally disconnect so he can fully engage in the fantasy state that he is creating. (Remember what we learned from our previous conversation of internal sexuality, that lust is always sin.)

For some men in this camp, the same fantasy of a particular sex act (for example, oral sex) is used over and over again with a woman who really wants to be sexual with him. Often he chooses the same type of fantasy woman (a particular race, a specific shape or a certain age woman). Any woman outside of his particular focus is less than interesting to him.

Others in this camp can be completely opposite in their choices. They are more interested in variety. They believe there shouldn't be any boundaries to their sexual fantasies and will objectify almost anyone in their fantasy state. For them, any sex act (legal or not) is acceptable and stimulating to them.

Although the fantasy isn't real, the object of the fantasy does whatever you want, whenever you want, always wants more, never asks for money, doesn't have children, never gets tired of you and, above all, really likes having sex with you. This fantasy is a sham, and the women in it aren't real.

However, if a man engages in an object-type of self sex and develops a neuropathic chemical reinforcement in his brain, it will affirm to him that object-type sex is chemically awesome. The desire to repeat this disconnected sex increases with the frequency in which he participates in this behavior.

Not only is this man disconnected during his sexual acts with himself, he is also reinforcing some pretty powerful, though unrealistic, belief systems about sex. The following is a list of some of the things men have placed in their fantasies.

Fantasy Ideas

- Sex is only with beautiful women.

- Sex is only with women who are in shape and have no fat.

- Women want sex all the time.

- Women think about sex all the time.

- The woman does all the work.

- Nothing is demanded of me but to receive sex (not give).

- Sex is all about me and what I want.

- I never hear "no" when it comes to sex.

- There is no good reason not to have sex.

- I am the center of the world, and the world revolves around me. Women are here to do as I ask.

- Women want to be degraded and talk dirty.

The list can go on and on for the man in this category, with many destructive attitudes ruling his disconnected fantasy state. Remember that most of these sexual beliefs and attitudes are formed when you are the most self-centered creature in the world—an adolescent male. Adolescents don't think about much more than themselves, their bodies, their friends and their life. It is easy to see why an adolescent male would create such a fantasy world.

The physical reality is that this disconnected fantasy state gets reinforced neurologically each time a young man indulges in his fantasy world. Some men can keep this type of sexuality strictly in fantasy, but others try to turn these fantasies into reality.

The result of the fantasy world is another issue. If the fantasy to which a man is disconnecting becomes illegal, degrading or deviant, it is more than likely that he will experience sexual self-shame. He may know masturbating to this fantasy is wrong or unhealthy, but he will eventually get stuck in the chemical rush with which he is rewarded afterward. It feels good, but it's wrong, and so he often feels confused.

Within the Type C disconnected camp there are great differences in the internal and external sexuality involved. When disconnecting during masturbation, the only point of similarity between men is ejaculation. Otherwise, the differences vary so widely that they are not related to the same internal experience at all.

The common issue with this form of masturbation is that lust is a big part of the act. For this reason, the man with Type C masturbation often feels guilt, shame and disconnection from God. Unfortunately, Type C masturbation is what most have experienced and many have possibly repented of repeatedly.

For many adult men who grew up in the sexual revolution, this is probably your experience. Sadly, Christian men and non-Christian men were both educated sexually by *Playboy*, not their fathers or godly men in the church.

It's just in recent years that men are reclaiming this area for their sons. Our video *Shepherding Your Sons Sexually* sells everywhere because of the desire men have to give more to their sons than their fathers gave to them.

From the above discussion, we understand that men do masturbate differently. Because the meanings of the word *masturbation* can differ so radically in men's experience, the word no longer defines the issue clearly. That is why I like to ask my clients if they are engaging in Type A, B or C masturbation. It gives us a way to talk in much clearer terms regarding masturbation.

THE MASTURBATION PLOT THICKENS

Now that we have an understanding of terms regarding the different types of masturbation, we can proceed. What happens when a Type B masturbator grows up and becomes a pastor, Christian counselor or Bible professor? Because he is coming from a purity perspective, he will not project lust, objectification or things like this into his message about masturbation. That was not a part of his experience. And he will rarely offer guidelines about avoiding fantasy, for that was not part of his experience either. So his message about masturbation will be basically that it's OK to masturbate.

We understand that men do masturbate differently.

Men who are Type C masturbators, listening to this Type B pastor, think that this Christian leader is giving them permission not to feel bad about the way they masturbate. So a Type C masturbator comes home from a Type B masturbator's conference thinking it is OK for him to keep masturbating with fantasy the way he has been. The C masturbator doesn't masturbate without lust, and therefore sins, but because of the message he heard, he now believes this is OK.

81

Inversely, when Type C masturbators become pastors, Christian counselors and Bible professors, their past experience dictates that all masturbation is lustful; therefore, all masturbation is sin. They proclaim the message that masturbation is always sin regardless of whether you're twelve or seventy years old. The problem with this message is that it rarely includes practical solutions on how to overcome such habits.

The above scenarios show why the lack of awareness regarding the different types of masturbation can result in a message that keeps men confused about the whole issue. To further clarify this complicated issue, we need to continue our rocky journey through an explanation of different patterns of masturbation. Not only do men masturbate differently; they also have different patterns of masturbation.

PATTERNS OF MASTURBATION

In this section, I want to help you pinpoint your pattern of masturbation. Before you can move to a place that you define as sexually successful, you must identify where you currently are.

CONNECTED PATTERNS (TYPE B)

- *Connected masturbation with occasional pattern:* This is a man who stays connected but occasionally will masturbate. The masturbation usually occurs during his wife's pregnancy or illness, long business trips or some other circumstance that makes relational sex not possible with his wife.

- *Connected masturbation with regular pattern:* This man may masturbate with a more than occasional frequency, such as monthly; however, he will stay connected throughout the masturbation experience, with no use of fantasy or other Type C behavior.

DISCONNECTED PATTERNS (TYPE C)

- *Disconnected masturbation with binge pattern:*
  This man masturbates quite often to fantasy, pornography or the objectification of others. Sometimes it may be every other week. It may be several times over a period of a few days. Or it may occur weeks or months apart from the previous episode.

- *Disconnected masturbation with regular pattern:*
  This man masturbates with a regular pattern, doing so during the times when he travels or his wife leaves the house for a night. This pattern may occur weekly more or less, but definitely has a regular frequency. The pattern may include slightly more or less sex than he typically has with his wife.

- *Disconnected masturbation with addictive pattern:*
  This adult man masturbates regularly, several times a week. His frequency of masturbation is equal to or greater than the sex with his wife. He has tried to stop without long-term success. He feels driven to masturbate regularly even when it doesn't make sense to him or to his internal moral code.

Whichever pattern you developed earlier in your life, or what pattern you currently practice, was probably acquired without identifying it by a name or having adequate information surrounding the behavior. As a typical young man, most of your masturbation thoughts, values and beliefs probably began during high school years or even earlier. Then as you grew older, you tried to make adjustments to reality.

Now, as a responsible adult, you need to decide whether or not you're going to masturbate. If so, then you need to decide if you are going to masturbate in a connected manner or disconnected manner. In my professional experience, I rarely find that Type C masturbators typically become Type B masturbators. Be careful not to deceive yourself.

You will also have to look at the frequency and the proportion of your masturbation behavior in comparison to connected sex with your wife. To help you with your evaluation, we will discuss this one final, but very important, issue: masturbation and marriage. This is a significant issue for the man who wants to be successful and wants to address masturbation in an intelligent and adult-like manner. Think through what you have read so far. You now have more information to make better choices for your future.

MASTURBATION AND MARRIAGE

When you marry, you make a huge commitment of yourself to another person. Often you don't even begin to understand the depth of your commitment until after a decade or so of being married.

In adjusting to this commitment, you may run into the issue of "ours" vs. "mine." For instance, in the area of finances, do you decide to have a joint account in which all money is "ours," or do you choose to have separate accounts, "mine" and "yours"?

Sex also represents a growth issue similar to finances. Prior to marriage, your consideration is "my" sexuality. In marriage, there is the consideration of "our" sexuality. Do you grow to the point where all sex is "our" sex, or do you feel entitled to your own sex without her knowledge?

The Scriptures will help give needed guidelines for our discussion. The apostle Paul wrote:

> Therefore, I urge you, brothers, in view of God's mercy, to offer your bodies as living sacrifices, holy and

pleasing to God—this is your spiritual act of worship.
—ROMANS 12:1

Since your penis is part of your body, God has ultimate authority over it, according to the Scriptures. The Scriptures also teach that your wife has authority in your sexuality:

> The husband should fulfill his marital duty to his wife, and likewise the wife to her husband. The wife's body does not belong to her alone but also to her husband. In the same way, the husband's body does not belong to him alone but also to his wife. Do not deprive each other except by mutual consent and for a time, so that you may devote yourselves to prayer. Then come together again so that Satan will not tempt you because of your lack of self-control.
> —1 CORINTHIANS 7:3–5

According to Paul, your wife has more authority over your sexuality, including masturbation, than you do. In this context, God is the first, your wife is the second and you are the third owner of your penis.

When you marry, you make a huge commitment of yourself to another person.

For some of you reading this, it's the first time you've been challenged about your sexuality not being just "yours." Is it solely yours to do with as you please? Is your sexual organ just for you, or was it really designed for your wife? Did the Creator of sex have in mind "me sex" for your whole life? You will have to decide for yourself whether your sexuality is "yours" or "ours" in marriage.

Does your wife have the right to know fully what you are doing sexually? When you walked down the aisle, was that the end of the "me sex" and the beginning of the "we sex"?

Typically this is not even considered nor thought about by men, but it certainly is by women.

Women generally think that when they marry a man their body belongs 100 percent to that man. They can't even conceive the "me sex" attitude, especially if the woman is typically available for sex. I believe that men who have disconnected masturbation (Type C habits) often view their sexuality as "me sex." They think that even though they are married, it's still OK to have a secret sexual life, so to speak.

Can you imagine sitting down with your wife to a nice meal at a restaurant and saying, "I've decided that 70 percent of our savings belongs just to me, so I'm going to move it into my name next week. OK, honey?" Even better, at the same restaurant, imagine telling your wife that 30 percent of your sexual expression is going to be with yourself from this time forward.

This is a decision you must make. Is your body 50 percent yours and 50 percent your wife's? Do you get 90 percent and she gets 10 percent? Do you get 30 percent and she gets 70 percent? You will have to decide and then let your wife know your decision.

Unfortunately, many men are not honest about their sexuality with themselves or with their wives. Men involved in masturbation, porn, fantasy and objectification of others rarely tell their wife that they are sharing their sexuality with others. If you truly want to know what you currently believe, take a minute and look at the percentage of masturbation, pornography usage and fantasy life that you involve yourself in that you don't tell your wife about. Take that number and ratio it over the times you have connected sex with her. How did you do? Are you a 100 percent type of guy where all sexuality is with her and she knows about anything else? Are you a 90 percent guy with 10 percent to yourself, or is it 50 percent for each of you? Did your wife show up in the minority of your sexual activity?

Knowing where you are sexually is important in determining your future sexual success. I have learned in my professional experience that secrecy and dishonesty in any area of your life does not lend itself to success in that area.

Personally, I believe the Scriptures teach that for a healthy marriage and sexual success, *all* of your sexuality must belong to you and your wife. Neither do I condone Type C masturbation or masturbation that takes the place of sex with your spouse. For women, the root problem of these issues is dishonesty.

HONESTY IS THE ISSUE

Most of the wives with whom I have counseled really don't understand the whole masturbation thing at all. The problem as they see it is lying. Women cannot get it; to them lying is the number one sin you can commit. They realize that their spouse will fall into doing some sin at some point in life—we all do; we're human. So why lie about it? That just may start a war.

When you lie to a woman, you might as well have called her the ugliest name that you can think of. Women take lying as a personal affront. Honestly, I can't say that I understand their reaction perfectly myself, but I can tell you from many years of experience as a therapist that it is real.

You may think that she has never asked you about your masturbation habits, so you have never lied to her about them. Unfortunately, only men think this way. She would think, *If you never told me, why didn't you? If you're really OK with what you're doing in private, why not tell me?*

If both of you sit down and agree that it's OK for you to have a sexual behavior without her, then she should be fine with knowing the truth. At least she knows, and she had a vote in the process. Remember, as with your financial arrangements, it is her sexuality you're "spending," not just yours. After you come to agreement about your sexual behavior, when you come home from a trip you can be as open and honest about your self-sex experience as you are about the rest of the experiences you had on the trip.

If this sounds too strange for you to do, then you may have made a sexual decision for yourself that is not part of your mutual agreement and remains secretive. If you can't be honest with your wife about your total sexual expression, then you probably need to evaluate the reason for your ongoing lies to your wife. It might help to ask yourself how you would feel to find out that your wife has a secret financial, sexual or other private area of her life that you know nothing about.

> # When you lie to a woman, you might as well have called her the ugliest name that you can think of.

Some women don't want to know if you masturbate, but giving them the choice to know is an honest position. Ask your wife, "Do you want to know if I masturbate? Do you want to know if I view pornography or fantasize about others when I masturbate?" Then, instead of you making these choices for her and having an ongoing secret in your relationship, she can voice her opinions and make a joint decision with you.

Some of you may believe you already know your wife's position on these issues and that makes you unwilling to expose your secret. If she doesn't get a choice and you continue to actively withhold complete information, it will probably blow up in your face in a big way down the road. Remember, her Father is God, and just because you won't tell doesn't mean He won't tell her for you.

If you're lying to your spouse, it isn't going to be good for your future sexual success. Secrets kill intimacy and affect sexuality. Your secret sex may be what is keeping you from having full three-dimensional sex with your wife, which will be your best sexual experience ever. If you masturbate while having a willing wife upstairs, you need to consider the choice you are making. Sexually healthy men, given the choice between their spouse who loves them and a fantasy, will choose the real woman.

I encourage you at least to give her the choice regarding how much of your sexuality is hers and how much of your sexuality is just for you. Honesty is the best policy when it comes to being sexually successful.

Some men will tell me that they "only fantasize" about her! I have heard this many times in my office. Typically I will ask such a man what his fantasy wife wants to do in his fantasy. Is she more sexual in fantasy than reality? Does she say things you have never heard her say in reality? Is she willing to do more or different types of sex in fantasy than in reality? If the answer to these questions is "yes," then you have "Wife A" and "Wife B." Wife A is the real one with kids to raise, a house to manage, perhaps an outside job and who occasionally gets sick, has cycles and doesn't always like you. Wife B is the one in your fantasies.

The problem is that if Wife B is giving your brain regular chemical reinforcement, then your brain will get really frustrated with your real wife (Wife A) because she is not as much fun. So be careful not to set up dual-brain reinforcement with the same face and body; you could get really confused.

When you have the conversation with your wife about masturbation, make sure you explain the difference between connected and disconnected masturbation, along with the frequency of it in your life, so that she understands what you are talking about. Many wives will not have an experiential template for these sexual behaviors. It would be good to evaluate your behavior by asking yourself some specific questions such as those that follow.

Questions to Ask Yourself
Before Masturbating

1. Am I trying to medicate a feeling?

2. Am I confused about what I am feeling?

3. Do I feel I can't wait forty-eight to seventy-two hours to masturbate?

4. Am I responding to a picture, movie or fantasy?

5. Am I violating a boundary that I originally set for myself?

6. Do I have a spouse?

7. Do I plan to fantasize during masturbation?

8. Will I feel badly about myself afterwards?

9. The last time I did this, did it send me on a binge of acting out?

10. Will I want to keep this a secret?

11. Am I using this as a stress release?

12. Am I a "B" or "C" masturbator?

By posing the above questions, I am in no way recommending masturbation behavior. I understand that some men will decide to masturbate, and I feel these questions will help them clarify the issue for them. They can help you decide whether or not to masturbate. If you have more "yes" than "no" answers, when you do choose to masturbate you might want to think through your motives or even talk to someone else about it.

Remember, you can become sexually successful regardless of your past choices regarding masturbation. Some of you may need to do some work on these issues. Some of you reading this book will make that decision. Others of you believe that these issues are not a problem for you at this point.

So, based on your present choices, what's it going to be like for you in the future? Decided yet? Consider these questions:

- Are you having connected masturbation?

- Are you having disconnected masturbation?

- Are you masturbating?

- Are you occasionally masturbating?

- Are you binge-masturbating?

- Are you having regular masturbating patterns?

- Are you being honest with your wife about the frequency and type of fantasy?

- Are you being dishonest with your wife about the frequency and type of fantasy?

- What percentage of your sexuality is "ours"?
  _____ percent

- What percentage is solely "yours"?
  _____ percent

These are some of the choices you face as you desire to be sexually successful. You are an adult and can't blame anyone else for your choices. They are important, as is the saving of money or spending it, having children or not having children, and choosing what you will do for a career.

You can make great choices for your sexual success. I hope this in-depth discussion on the issue of masturbation makes you a more informed decision-maker. If you struggle in this area occasionally, establish some male accountability. If you feel addicted to masturbation, follow the guidelines for getting free from addiction offered in the earlier section of the book where we address the topic of major battlefronts.

SIX

The Seductress

A very important conversation about male sexuality is the discussion of the issue of seduction. The destructive power of seduction can lead a good man down a wrong path and cause him to lose every good thing for which he was created.

It is interesting to me that the wisest man in the world, King Solomon, gave priority to the discussion of seduction in the Book of Proverbs. The first four chapters of Proverbs exalt wisdom and encourage everyone to seek wisdom above all. Then in chapter five, the folly of adultery is addressed, complete with graphic detail of how an adulterous woman can cost a man everything. By its placement, we can conclude that the folly of adultery is the number one threat to having wisdom. And without wisdom we cannot hope to become sexually successful.

God's Ten Commandments support this conclusion. The first four commandments teach us that our relationship with God is primary. The fifth and sixth commandments teach us how to treat our parents and not to kill other people. The seventh commandment forbids committing adultery, and the last commandment reinforces that prohibition, asking us not to lust after or covet another man's wife. (See Exodus 20.)

So I am in good company in giving priority to a discussion of seduction. This is especially for our Western culture, which teaches little boys that girls are made of "sugar and spice and everything nice." The effects of this false picture of women are compounded by our modern feminist culture, which portrays men on prime-time television as dumb, needing women to continually straighten them out.

Most information we receive about women declares them to be essentially good. That is true of most women. Many are selfless in parenting, patient, kind and loyal in marriage. I personally have a great wife who is an incredibly good woman. Though most women are great, there are some who do not have good intentions toward men.

The destructive power of seduction can lead a good man down a wrong path.

The reality is that women are people, and all people have the potential for good and evil. The Scriptures record both the good and evil of people throughout the Old and New Testaments. The Old Testament records the beauty, submission and wisdom of Sarah in her relationship with Abraham. Such beautiful character traits are also illustrated in the story of Ruth by her loyalty to Naomi. And who can forget the queen of all that is good—Esther! The Old Testament preserves the record as well of some women who were not good, like Delilah, who sacrificed a man who loved her for money. King Ahab's wife, Jezebel, is another terrible example of a woman ruled by evil intentions for selfish gain.

The New Testament presents Mary, the mother of Jesus, as a wonderful example of a good woman. Mary Magdalene,

Jesus' friend, is also an excellent example, as was Lydia the seller of purple and Dorcas, who gave sacrificially of herself to love and help others. The wicked life of Herodias, the wife of Herod who plotted to kill John the Baptist, is also recorded there. And in Revelation 2:18–29 another Jezebel is described as a false prophetess who was leading God's people into sexual immorality in the church of Thyatira.

I say all this to demonstrate that God's Word presents both men and women as they are—living lives for good or evil. For example, Proverbs 5 and 7 describe the power of the evil of seduction we are about to discuss. And Proverbs 31 gives us one of the greatest descriptions of the virtuous woman.

Let me add here that I have no ax to grind with women—not even seductresses. I have authored several books and tape series to help women who have suffered the effects of men's sexual addiction issues. I have also written two books to help women who need to heal from their own female sexual addictions. It is my great desire to see all people, regardless of gender, heal from sexual sins.

In addition, because I want to be biblically balanced, I feel the need to warn men regarding the seductress who can be found not only in the world, but also in the church. This type of woman needs to be clearly identified and avoided so that you can live happily ever after with God and your precious wife.

PROVERBS 7—THE POWER OF SEDUCTION

In the following pages I will introduce you to the mind and heart of the seductress. As a young man, I met this type of woman many times. As a therapist, I have happily witnessed the seductress heal and recover. But I have also heard hundreds of stories of men who were ravaged by her.

Our discussion of the seductress will be based on a verse-by-verse commentary of Proverbs 7, using the New

International Version. If you have your Bible handy, I would encourage you to read your translation as well.

A FATHER'S WISDOM

> My son, keep my words and store up my commands within you. Keep my commands and you will live; guard my teachings as the apple of your eye. Bind them on your fingers; write them in the tablet of your heart. Say to wisdom, "You are my sister," and call understanding your kinsman; they will keep you from the adulteress, from the wayward wife with her seductive words.
>
> —PROVERBS 7:1–5

As King Solomon addresses his son, he addresses all men who read his words. He tells us to seek wisdom, to love wisdom enough to be practical about it. He encourages us to write down the words of wisdom that will guard him from evil. This is good advice. The older I get the more I need to write important things down that I want to remember.

He tells us that if we keep the commands of wisdom, we will be safe from the adulterous, wayward wife and her seductive words. In recovery literature there is a concept called "principles above personalities." This concept is very helpful to teach how you can so get caught up in, or attached to, a personality (especially a woman's) that you throw away wisdom and common sense. You may even choose to violate the principle of God's Word that teaches, "Thou shall not commit adultery."

We need to love God, love His Word and base our lives on principles instead of following a hippie-based culture that says, "If it feels good, do it" or "Love the one you're with!" (I personally think they would be more honest to say, "Lust the one you're with!")

When you live a life based in principles of wisdom, the seductress loses any power she could have over you. But if your heart is open to lust or curiosity, she will always direct you down a path of heartbreak and hardship.

A FOOLISH YOUTH

> At the window of my house I looked out through the lattice. I saw among the simple, I noticed among the young men, a youth who lacked judgment. He was going down the street near her corner, walking along in the direction of her house at twilight, as the day was fading, as the dark of night set in.
>
> —PROVERBS 7:6–9

I like the way the writer sets the scene for us in these verses. He makes himself the proverbial bystander looking at another man's life. The young man he sees is simple and lacking in judgment. Remember, in ancient times when this was written there were no streetlights to light the path after dark. At night people stayed inside to keep both warm and safe. This young man was not expecting to be home by dark.

I like the statement "He was . . . walking along in the direction of her house" because it places some responsibility on the young man for his actions. He chose to walk that road. I believe at best that he was naive. He might not have been expecting to seek out sex that night.

Maybe he was just curious. Maybe he heard some other guys talking about their experiences down at the corner after dark. Scripture does not answer these questions. What I can tell you is that I have heard countless stories of men who, like this young man, suffered the consequences of taking that first curious step down the wrong path.

For example, Jerry would surf the Internet after his wife was in bed. Jerry soon met someone online in a chat room and grew very fond of her, even to the point of wanting to leave his wife and family to be with her. The woman refused to meet Jerry until he officially left his wife.

When Jerry told his wife he wanted a divorce, his wife

asked if she could go with him to meet this other woman. For whatever reason, Jerry agreed. They arrived together at the house where this woman lived. When they knocked on the door, a homosexual man greeted them. Needless to say, this deception shocked Jerry. He sought professional help and gratefully returned to his wife.

I can tell many sad stories about numerous Christian men who were traveling on business trips and visited a hotel bar without any intention of having sex. There they met a woman who was looking for a naive and simple man. One thing led to another, and adultery was consummated. The same story is told by Christian men who have gone to a strip club or massage parlor and encountered a seductress there. In all of these cases the men were "walking in the direction of her house." Most of these incidences occur "after hours" and in the wrong section of town or in a place where a man of principle wouldn't go.

The seductress introduced

> Then out came a woman to meet him, dressed like a
> prostitute and with crafty intent.
> —Proverbs 7:10

The major player in this drama is now introduced. She is the seductress. The author tells us a little about her outward appearance and her inward intent. She is dressed like a prostitute. Applied to our culture, this woman would be one who dressed seductively—tight pants, cleavage showing, lots of attention paid to perfecting her hair and makeup. Unfortunately, since men in America worship women's bodies, they could look for her anywhere—the gym, grocery store, work or even church.

This is her "outside." The seductress sends out obvious sexual energy by the way she dresses and looks. Female sex addicts admit that they consciously choose specific outfits in order to hook their prey. One female therapist who counsels a group of female sex addicts asked the ladies to come to one meeting wearing a seductive outfit they would use to conquer a man. Some of the women wore sophisticated suits, one wore an exercise outfit, and another wore tight jeans and a revealing top. Though all were dressed very differently, they chose clothes that they knew would be a weapon for seduction.

The "inside" part of the seductress introduced in Proverbs 7:10 reveals a heart filled with "crafty intent." Some women really do embrace evil and an inappropriate sexual intent. Part of my own healing required my dealing with the women I was sexual with between the ages of sixteen and nineteen. These women were much older than I. Some were married, and all of them definitely had evil intent toward me. They wanted to use me sexually and then throw me away.

Sex was a only game to them, which made me a target. Many guys who have had similar experiences actually feel they "got lucky." What they got was being used by seductresses in a way that could sometimes qualify as sexual abuse.

To be forewarned about the crafty intentions of the seductress, whether she is married or single, Christian or non-Christian, is a good preparation for winning the battle against her. I can't tell you how many young men have confided to me they had to break up with a Christian woman because she was pressuring them into sex. Know this: To a seductress, men are not considered in any way special; they are just her sex partner.

HER CHARACTER

> She is loud and defiant, her feet never stay at home;
> now in the street, now in the squares, at every corner
> she lurks.
>
> —PROVERBS 7:11–12

The behavior and attitudes of a seductress are clearly

described here. This woman does whatever she pleases; she is not submissive but "loud and defiant." This may not be obvious to you when you first meet her. Though she may appear demure, maybe even quiet and spiritual at first, her inward rebellion will reveal itself as you develop a relationship with her. She likes to be about town, so to speak. She will not show interest in responsible activities of a virtuous woman to make a home or raise children.

I like the way the writer describes her locale: "at every corner she lurks." I think this was included to help men be aware that this type of woman does exist in your community. Don't be fooled into thinking you live in Mayberry. The seductress is a reality in every locale and needs to be guarded against. Men in ministry, this is crucial! The strongest of Christians could be fooled into believing in her, including other women!

Catching her prey

> She took hold of him and kissed him and with a brazen face she said . . .
>
> —Proverbs 7:13

The seductress readily reveals her crafty intent; she is not afraid to initiate the next step. Put a modern face on this situation. You're flirting with a coworker and find yourself alone with her. She grabs and kisses you. This is the edge of the hook that goes into a man's spirit, soul and body. All of a sudden your brain turns off and your body ignites.

Sexually the seductress is confident. She intuitively understands what prostitutes know: All men want to be wanted. She knows that as a man your deepest longing is to feel desired by a woman sexually. That's why she talks with a "brazen" or shameless face. She knows what she's doing. She has studied victims like you before.

It's even harder for you if your marriage is less than wonderful. When your wife sincerely says she desires you, that hole in your heart is filled so completely that no other woman's voice can be anything but distasteful. You become especially vulnerable to the seductress if you are not feeling wanted in your marriage. For men in this situation, I would recommend my book *Intimacy: A 100-Day Guide to Lasting Relationships* and the videos *The Best Sex of Your Life, for Men Only* and *The Best Sex of Your Life, for Women Only*. (You may order the videos at www.intimatematters.com or by calling Heart to Heart Counseling Center at 719-278-3708.) These materials will strengthen your marriage so that if you meet a seductress, you will be able to withstand her craftiness.

Now we are going to delve deeper into the seductress's mind-set. Knowing what she says to the man whom she is victimizing is priceless because it informs you of her true heart.

FULFILLING RELIGIOUS VOWS

"I have fellowship offerings at home; today I fulfilled my vows."

—PROVERBS 7:14

She is spiritual! She makes reference to fulfilling a religious vow. According to Leviticus 7:12–16, such fellowship offerings were to be eaten by family members. Now what man would turn down a free meal with a sexy lady who is attracted to him?

The meal may seem innocent or religious, but it's not. She is luring and seducing him to her place. This would be comparable to a woman saying, "Come over the day after Thanksgiving; my husband and kids are gone." Better yet, "We had a prayer meeting last night, and I've got some leftover food. Wouldn't you like a tasty snack?" If you think this sounds ridiculous, let me assure you I personally know of men falling for lines weaker than this.

> "So I came out to meet you; I looked for you and have found you!"
>
> —Proverbs 7:15

The seductress makes you feel so special. She uses the word *you* three times in one sentence. I feel a little uncomfortable any time someone tries to make me think I'm special. When you are on a business trip and a woman takes a "special interest" in you and what you do, my advice is to run for the hills!

You don't need a strange woman telling you how special you are.

None of us are that "special." You have a life. You may be married and have kids. You don't need a strange woman telling you how special you are. She will make you "feel" that you're special, smart, handsome and appreciated. Remember, if a woman who is not your wife (or fiancée) is trying to convince you that you're special, you are being warmed up to be fried, no matter who she is.

SPECIAL TREATMENT

> "I have covered my bed with colored linens from Egypt. I have perfumed my bed with myrrh, aloes and cinnamon. Come, let's drink deep of love till morning; let's enjoy ourselves with love!"
>
> —Proverbs 7:16–18

Oh baby! Now you are so "special" that this woman is also going to provide you with a sexual encounter like you have never had before. She definitely is playing on your fantasy of "the special interlude." Just look at the sell: special sheets and special incense or aromas.

She is going to sell you the illusion that forbidden fruit

is better. Different maybe, but is it better? No way! The price you pay for that encounter—the rest of your life will become a living hell. But I'm getting ahead of myself.

This verse is so important to understand: "Come, let's drink deep of love till morning; let's enjoy ourselves with love!" The seductress believes that sex is love. But she is not offering you love—just a one-night stand. Love involves lifelong commitment and monogamy. It means working out differences and serving each other for a lifetime, till death do you part. Love is not a quick jump in the sack.

If any woman tries to sell you on sex outside of marriage, no matter who she is or how much of a "Christian" she seems to be, run from her. She is a seductress. Nothing good can happen here.

I know it's hard to believe that there are women in the church who are seductresses, but it is true. So stay alert! To be sexually successful for your entire life you must stay on guard against the seductress.

"YOU ARE SAFE."

> "My husband is not at home; he has gone on a long journey. He took his purse filled with money and will not be home till full moon."
>
> —PROVERBS 7:19–20

Here she throws you the line that there are no consequences to fear because her husband is gone. There is no immediate threat. "Come on, buddy, nobody will know. It will be great." Doesn't that sound like the devil himself? Of course, she never mentions God's judgment that will come on your life or the consequences that are sure to follow. She focuses only on immediate pleasure. She reassures you that nothing bad is going to happen.

POWERFUL PERSUASION

With persuasive words she led him astray; she seduced

him with her smooth talk. All at once he followed her like an ox going to the slaughter, like a deer stepping into a noose.

—PROVERBS 7:21–22

The seductress's most powerful weapon is her words. That's why it's not good to even talk to her. Many men have found the longer they talk to her, the weaker they become and the easier she can conquer them. Her words are smooth, kind, enticing and full of promises for immediate pleasure. They are earmarks of a seductress.

The fact that the man described in this passage fell for her lies says it all. He didn't follow God's principles or wisdom. He followed *her*. Our naive man has now made himself a victim of the seductress; it will cost him his life. Many men have wept in my office from the pain they suffered after awakening from the fog of their lustful encounter with a willing seductress.

The writer of the Proverbs gives us another lengthy passage that warns of this kind of pain and destruction. He also gives insight into the attitudes and rebellion that motivate the man who becomes her victim:

> Keep to a path far from her, do not go near the door of her house, lest you give your best strength to others and your years to one who is cruel, lest strangers feast on your wealth and your toil enrich another man's house. At the end of your life you will groan, when your flesh and body are spent. You will say, "How I hated discipline! How my heart spurned correction! I would not obey my teachers or listen to my instructors. I have come to the brink of utter ruin in the midst of the whole assembly."
>
> —PROVERBS 5:8–14

The men I've counseled who have committed adultery all confirm the truth of this scripture. Inevitably they testify to the loss of their wealth and their toil to enrich another man as they describe the devastating outcome of their decisions. This can easily happen in a divorce where your assets go into child support and alimony—and your ex-wife's new husband's boats and cars—all paid for with your hard-earned money.

The enemy's plan is to use the seductress to strip you of your destiny, your wife and your role as the father of your children. Christian men have somehow been lulled into a stupor sexually. The false sense of men's sexual entitlement that motivates them to engage in pornography, masturbation and other wrong behavior leaves them easy prey for the seductress.

The seductress's most powerful weapon is her words.

Take heed to these scriptures, and guard your heart and your life from the seductress; she is death. Her intent is to kill what you love, leave you and then move on to another victim. Remember that many are the victims she has brought down, which means you're not as special as she would make you think. She is bent on massive spiritual, social and financial destruction.

You can totally escape her trap by loving God, pursuing wisdom and living a life based upon principles rather than seeking immediate pleasure. Again let me warn you that when you see any female displaying the signs we discussed, run from her.

In a culture that promotes female sexuality in every form of media, temptation can be lurking everywhere. But our God is everywhere as well, and if we walk with Him, He will deliver us. Be wise, be careful and be blessed!

SEVEN

Creating a Sexually Successful Brain

Having a sexually successful brain is crucial to having sexual success. If your brain remains dual- or multi-focused as we discussed in chapter two, sexual success will continue to elude you. But regardless of the level of success you are at right now, if you embrace and practice the principles we will discuss in the following chapters, you will be more sexually successful than ever before in your life.

As we begin our discussion of these principles, keep in mind the "ring the bell, feed the dog" analogy. When you have an orgasm, the highest level of endorphins and enkephalins that you can receive are sent to the excitement center of your brain. Whatever you are looking at when you ejaculate is that to which you will sexually glue or to which your sexuality will be attached. You will begin to have a strong sexual desire for whatever the image, object or person that you view regularly when you ejaculate.

Men who have a dual-focused or multi-focused sexual brain get distracted throughout the day trying to get better looks at women they are ogling. Recently, I was talking

107

to an old client who made a lot of money in the porn industry. He definitely had a multi-focused brain. Over the years his brain has seen and reinforced hundreds of thoughts and images.

After receiving counseling and embracing healthy principles of sexuality, he said, "I can't believe how truly free I feel. I don't have to lust after every woman that's in my vision. I don't have to lust after her in my mind or think about what sex with her would be like. I don't disconnect from reality when I am at restaurants anymore with my fiancée." He was so happy that he had been able to recondition his multi-focused brain.

RETRAINING YOUR BRAIN

One of the areas we specialize in at Heart to Heart Counseling Center is sexual addiction. We have offered free weekly newsletters through our website since 1994 (available at www.sexaddict.com). The site provides help for people who want answers for sexual addiction recovery and is the largest of its kind in the world. Currently tens of thousands of addicts and their wives are subscribers. In 1997, when we had about two thousand subscribers, we completed a survey for sex addicts who had been helped.

As you may know, there are hard-core sex addicts that utilize porn, sex, prostitutes and toys almost as diligently as working a part-time job. They see every woman as an object or just a body. They are preoccupied with sex in any way possible throughout the day. The sexual addict is the person who makes sexual comments about every woman that he knows, talks about the newest porn site that he found and, of course, tells only jokes that are sexually tainted.

We asked over two thousand sex addicts who subscribed to our newsletter to report to us the things that were most helpful to them during their recovery process. We did not provide any options to check off or leading questions to get a specific response. They were simply to write down what had helped them the most significantly.

STEP 1: THE RUBBER BAND TECHNIQUE

Their number one response was the fact that their wife stayed with them through the healing process. Their number two response to what was most helpful to them was *the rubber band technique*. It was voted even more helpful than support groups, recovery books or other tools that have been a great benefit in recovery. This exercise may appear very simplistic, but the results it brings are phenomenal.

To discover the benefits of this exercise for yourself, simply place a rubber band around your wrist for sixty to ninety days. Each time you have an inappropriate (non-relational) sexual thought, including a fantasy image or the objectifying of a woman, snap the rubber band on the inside of your wrist.

When you do this, neurologically your brain sees its stimulus (a woman), but instead of your brain getting a positive chemical reinforcement from enkephalins and endorphins, it receives a pain stimulus from the snapping of the rubber band. Over a period of a month or so, your brain no longer desires to feel that pain each time you sexually objectify a woman. It has been reconditioned.

This exercise represents basic behavior modification. Most of the sex addicts with whom I have counseled say that 80 percent of their double takes (looking back at women), rubbernecking (stretching to catch a better view) or objectifying of women shut down when they used this recovery tool. Many of these sex addicts say they gain about ten to fifteen hours a week for other activities after they curtail this behavior. Perhaps their victories will encourage you to try it for yourself.

Remember the "ring the bell, feed the dog" analogy. You can't change the "bell." God knows there are women everywhere. If you condition your brain to see them as objects, you will be preoccupied sexually with the "bell" all day long. But if through this simple exercise you choose to recondition your brain, you will be surprised how much free time you will gain, especially if you have a dual-focused or multi-focused brain. Although you can't change the situation (the bell), you can change your response.

Let's use another dog story to further explain the power of behavior modification. Suppose you had a puppy that was continually having an accident on the floor, and every time this happened you gave it a great big T-bone steak. The puppy would associate going on the floor with eating a steak. This pup is like your brain that associates getting a chemical buzz by sexually objectifying a woman. If you keep feeding the puppy T-bone steaks in this manner, you will have a very fat dog and a very messy house.

Most of you would get a newspaper and swat the pup that continually goes on the floor. When the pup connects going on the floor with a swat, it will stop going on the floor if it has any sense. The result: a dog of healthy weight and a clean home.

Many of you have been conditioning your brain for sexual gratification in this way for twenty, thirty, forty years or more. By rewarding the "pup" for wrong behavior, in reality you have been setting yourself up to have a dual-focused or a multi-focused brain. After thirty days of "swatting your dog" (snapping the rubber band), you will stop objectifying women and will be able to once again shut down the neuropathic reward system you have conditioned over time.

The multi-focused brain—depending on the frequency of reinforcement behaviors—may value object-type relationships more than relational ones. As a result, you make your wife feel unimportant and unloved. I've heard more than a thousand women complain about how unloved their dual-focused or multi-focused sexually brained husbands make them feel.

The good news is that even the most multi-focused brain

can feel his neuropathic conditioning process change after diligently practicing the rubber band technique. This is especially true for the man who is also choosing to change his primary sexual behavior from fantasy to relational. As he focuses on intimacy with his wife, he will begin to experience the highest chemical reward his body can produce. All his sexual rewards are being poured into a relational neuropathic outlet, which is continually growing stronger. His level of satisfaction increases each time he is intimate with his wife, and his sexual desire for her, and her alone, grows stronger.

STEP 2: THE THREE PRINCIPLES

From a "brain" perspective, the more people with whom you have sex and to whom you try to attach, the less you will feel attached to anyone. You will feel like the dog that continues to chase its tail and never catches it. A sexually successful brain is the one that attaches repeatedly to the same person, creating a chemical connection to that person that continually gets stronger. This is the reason couples who have had sex for thirty or forty years together say they are now enjoying the best sex of their lives.

Before we continue, let's review where we have been:

1. Remember the "ring the bell, feed the dog" theory.

2. Understand that your sexual release or ejaculation gives your brain the highest chemical rewards—endorphins and enkephalins.

3. Realize that your brain attaches to whatever it is that you look at during a sexual release.

4. It is a fact that the more variety of objects, fantasy or people you connect to, the more fractured your sexual focus and the less your sexual satisfaction. The more a consistent

relationship is reinforced, the more sexual
pleasure will be associated with that person.

It's up to you. You can choose to chase your tail sexually,
continually spinning in a myriad of unsatisfying directions,
or you can decide to have one person in your life.

One monogamous relationship will not only be more
satisfying, but it will also become more desirable over time
as well. Choosing to have relational sex and including the
three principles that follow will not only give you the best
neurological sex of your life, but it can also make you more
attracted to your wife.

When your brain thinks of sex, it will think of this person in your life, her eyes, her body and her voice. You can
etch such a strong, relationally connected neuro-pathway
to this person that your brain will be totally satiated with
just her. Begin implementing the following principles
today with your wife; you will begin to increase your sexual
attraction to and fulfillment with the person you love.

Principle #1: Eyes open. During sexual intercourse,
keep your eyes open and focused on your spouse. When
you get to the point of ejaculation, look into your spouse's
eyes. It will blow you away. This may seem awkward to you
or your spouse, especially if you have been experiencing a
disconnection during sex in the past. If you typically close
your eyes during release, you are not maximizing the
opportunity. If you fantasize during your sexual release,
you are attaching to the fantasy and not to your spouse.

If your spouse is disconnected as well during sex, which
may be a result of feeling alone during sex, that may be why
she is not as interested in sex as you wish she were.
Following this principle will attach you to your wife, and
she will become more satisfying to you the more you are
sexual together over the years.

Principle #2: Lights on. While making love, keep a light
on. It doesn't have to be bright; it can even be candlelight.

The point is, if it's so dark that you can't see your wife's eyes and body, then it doesn't matter whether you look at her or not. If you are always making love to her in the dark, then you're not neurologically or visually attaching to her. As a result, she will not become as sexually attractive to you.

Most women don't understand that a man attaches to his wife by looking at her. If she understood this, she would know that her physical appearance doesn't matter. Once you consistently attach to her person relationally, her body will become desirable regardless of its proportions.

Some women think of themselves as unattractive because they don't have "the perfect body." (Who does?) Great three-dimensional sex with your wife—body, mind and spirit—is possible for those who follow these principles of sexual success regardless of physical appearance.

The most beautiful couple in the world who is having multi-focused or disconnected sex will be much less satisfied sexually than a less attractive couple that follows the principles of sexual success. I have counseled many couples in my office who were physically and financially well to do and yet not sexually satisfied. Many of these young and beautiful couples were not even having sex together for months at a time.

So keep the lights on and look into each other's eyes, and you will attach to each other in a very satisfying way. Regardless of outward appearances, you will enjoy a sexually successful life.

Principle #3: Nurturing connection. As we have mentioned, sexual success engages your spirit, soul and body. If you accept the fact that sex is three-dimensional, and you decide to experience this phenomenon, you can expect a sexual experience that is satisfying and much more rewarding for the both of you.

However, when you are making love to your spouse and you are disconnected (in fantasy), you are engaging only your *body* in your sexual experience. Because of this reality, you and your spouse will feel less than satisfied with your sexual experience. Although it may be a somewhat physically satisfying experience for you, it will become harder and harder to talk your wife into being sexual again because you are both missing the spiritual and emotional components.

Imagine if your consistent behavior let your wife know she was going to be praised, nurtured and accepted every time you were together sexually. During this time she knew she would not be critiqued, compared or criticized. Don't you think she would want to be with you again and again? That will happen when you make sex a three-dimensional place where you nurture her spirit, soul and body.

If you accept the fact that sex is three-dimensional, you can expect a sexual experience that is satisfying.

Every woman differs in her likes and dislikes; however, most want to be touched in nonsexual areas before being sexual. Learn how to nurture your spouse spiritually and emotionally. Take responsibility for the other two-thirds (soul and spirit) of this special person in your life who is willing to be sexual with you. Learn to honor and connect to her. How you respond to her soul and spirit during sex is more important to most women than what you do with her body. She is turned on by closeness.

When you're making love to your wife, make an intentional effort to praise and nurture her. Go deeper than just complimenting her body. Speak to her spirit and soul during sex. You can become a great nurturer during your sexual experience by telling her how much you appreciate her in ways that aren't sexual. Tell her that you love her honesty, her strength and her intelligence. Tell her what her beauty does for you. Tell her she makes you feel masculine and that you love being with her.

What you say or don't say during your sexual experience goes deeper into her soul and spirit than any other words you say to her at any other time. When she is open to you sexually, she opens her entire being to you. If you use these vulnerable moments to complain about sex or to try to talk her into trying something new, you will be unsuccessful. The results of such lack of genuine nurturing have long-term effects with a pattern of ongoing sexual frustration for both of you. If you are silent with her during this time of openness and ignore her spirit and soul during sex, this pattern of emptiness will leave her unfulfilled.

Sex is a time for a verbal celebration of your wife. She needs that love, praise and connection. When you are sexual with her, if you honor all three parts of her being, more than likely you will have less difficulty with her lack of desire for sex.

Imagine what intimacy could be like if you and your spouse both learned how to receive the nurturing and connecting that your spirit and soul desires. Not only are you being touched physically, but you are also relating in a three-dimensional way that God created you to enjoy. Imagine what it would be like to feel wanted sexually by her regularly.

Most guys try to get their spouses to do this or that to have a multi-sensual experience. Imagine the joy of your soul being washed with praise and acceptance and your spirit being connected to by her. Imagine your brain on overload, receiving pleasure in all three dimensions at the same time. The resulting orgasm is satisfying all the way to the core of your being. And your sexually successful brain sends a triple hit attaching you to the woman to whom you are committed. This experience is normal for the man with a sexually successful brain; his brain receives the highest reward sexually and craves and aches to connect to his woman.

I promise that if you use these three principles for one

hundred days, you will never want to leave them. In all the years of my counseling practice, I have never had a client say they wanted sex the old way again after doing so. Once you taste sexual success, you can never be talked into anything less again.

EIGHT

What About Her?

Women are distinctly different from men, and for that I say, "Thank You, God." Women don't think, feel or experience life the same way you or I do, and throughout history, no man has been able to grasp fully what that really means.

I think women are a wonder with so much to offer in every area of life. Occasionally I have heard men in my office complain that their spouse was keeping them as a couple from being sexually successful. Some of the issues they are referring to come from not having the inside information concerning what women are about. Some men wonder why their spouse doesn't think and feel as they do. Some men get frustrated over these differences. Instead of trying to understand their wives and work with them the way they are, they try to change their wife. As a result, they end up hurting themselves. Be forewarned: This "her" discussion may get a bit sketchy if you try to move from point to point without connecting the dots.

WHAT MOTIVATES HER?

Generally speaking, your spouse is not primarily motivated by sight. This is a really good thing because your physical attributes between the ages of twenty and sixty can change dramatically. Sometimes your waist enlarges and the hair on your head falls out, while other hair begins to grow in strange places. Sometimes your flair for clothes diminishes, too. If women were motivated by sight, older men wouldn't be having much sex.

During counseling sessions when the question is raised about what makes a woman want to be sexual with her husband, most women affirm it *is when they feel close to him*. The key word in this sentence is *feel*. I know you may not want to hear that her moods or feelings control her sexual desire, but those are the facts.

Her general feelings about you will dynamically affect her sense of closeness toward you. She is not keeping score of your activities when you are together or apart, but rather she is evaluating how close your heart is to hers. It is important for you to understand how she processes her feelings about you.

A woman thinks about how things are going globally within the relationship. She contemplates the time you have shared together recently and how open the lines of communication have been. She reflects on how supportive you have been, if you have you kept your word and whether or not you have treated her with respect. These and many other thought processes influence her feelings toward you.

Please don't try to manipulate her with this information. This is not a check-off list for you to complete eight out of ten to obtain sexual success. It isn't that easy. This understanding will help you know how she processes her thoughts. These thoughts may be different for each woman and, to make it even more complicated, her thoughts may vary from day to day.

You may think this sounds strange and is difficult to understand. But to be fair, men process thoughts in ways that sound odd to women also. For example, when men walk into a room full of people, they automatically size up the situation to see how they measure up to the other guys in the room. In this way, men get a feel for what is expected of them and can assure themselves and their spouse that they are in control. Guys really do this! These episodes are similar to what a woman does when she globally checks you out to reassure herself of the place she has your life. If her conclusion is that everything is OK between her and you, she feels she can let her guard down and be intimate with you.

She is motivated by your emotional proximity to her just as you are motivated by her physical proximity to you. When you see her, you may feel a surge of sexual energy sweep over you. You know the feeling. It is called "sexual opportunity." So why not optimize the situation? It can also work that way for her if she has a sense of real connection to your heart. When she feels close to you she wants to be intimate.

Let me repeat: I am not selling a quick way to get sex. That doesn't exist. But generally speaking, if you can master the skills that increase intimacy, you can warm up the emotional climate in your relationship so that your wife will want to experience more of these special moments with you.

Some of you may be unwilling or unmotivated to change simply so she will feel close to you. Let's get practical here and use language that you may be able to relate to more. Almost every man reading this book has purchased an automobile. That beautiful new car came with guidelines that you were expected to follow to enjoy its optimum performance. One important guideline says you should change your oil every three thousand miles. You may complain, "That's not fair! Why in the world should I have to change my lifestyle to get under the hood of my car and get all dirty changing the oil, or worse, have to take it to a station where they charge me three times the cost of the oil and filter!"

Every guy knows what would happen if you whined about life not being fair and decided not to change the oil in your nice, shiny new car. Your beauty of a vehicle would run fine in the beginning, but slowly—almost inconspicuously—the engine would start reacting. That expensive engine of yours would begin to make funny noises and grinding sounds. There would come a day when the engine would get sluggish because you chose not to accept the reality that your car needed regular oil changes. The engine would eventually cough its final cough and freeze up.

> ## She is motivated by your emotional proximity to her just as you are motivated by her physical proximity to you.

Mechanics, lawyers and therapists all prosper from the behavior of guys who behave like this toward their cars and wives. Common sense and following instructions could have easily prevented what has now become a catastrophe. While the situation may still be salvageable, the solution is going to be quite expensive!

The better approach would have been to accept the way your automobile is made, and then change your lifestyle so that you can regularly and preventively take care of it. Likewise, because your wife has normal needs and desires, she will need regular "oiling"; she needs to be nurtured by you. If you choose not to do these things, it will be very difficult to have sexual success with the locked-up "engine" sleeping next to you.

Men, I have to shoot straight. You are basically responsible to maintain the connectedness with your wife. Scripture confirms this reality when it exhorts husbands to "love your wives, just as Christ loved the church and gave himself up for her" (Eph. 5:25). It was Christ who pursued the church to bring us into relationship with Him, not the other way around. When you follow these guidelines, life with your wife can work positively in your favor. If you choose not to, you can support the counseling industry in your local area. I want you to be sexually successful and to inherit all the land God has for you. For that to happen, you will have to decide to do what it takes to get there.

I know most men are not equipped to meet their wife's emotional needs intuitively, but there are skills you can learn that will enable you to do so. The more you understand her for who she is, the more likely you are to experience sexual success.

WHERE ARE THE BUTTONS?

I have heard many frustrated husbands in my office ask the question, "Where are the buttons?" Men are looking for the elusive "magical button" that will make their wife want to be sexual. Especially they want to find the button that says, "I want to have sex with you right now!"

You may spend years of your married life trying to discover that one hot button. Some men try rubbing their wife's feet, while others do the "back massage routine." Still others think that rubbing her head or combing her hair will prove to be the magic trick. Regardless of where you try to look for this button on the woman you are married and committed to, you may never find it.

Some men say there used to be a button in the beginning of their relationship. There was a formula that worked, a place where they touched her and something they said— then they were sexual. That's why they are wondering, "Where did that button go?"

Let me tell you the rest of Pavlov's story. Pavlov wanted to see if "ring the bell, feed the dog" would apply to humans. So while he was putting his young preschool-age daughter to bed, he decided to touch her back. As he did this she pulled up her one leg. He repeated this several times and every time he did, her leg went up. He thought he was onto something big until his young daughter asked, "Daddy, why is it when I pull my leg up that one minute later you touch my back?" She thought she was training him to touch her back, while he thought he was training her to pull up her leg. He laughed and realized that the apple doesn't fall far from the tree.

Why did I tell you this story? The reason is simple. Early in your marriage relationship you probably thought you found the "button." You may have thought, *If I touch here and say, "I really love you," wham! I'm going to have sex.* So you think to yourself, *I'm a smart guy. I know how to manipulate this engine to give me what I want.*

However, years later, you are wondering why that same touch and three gushes of "I really love you" don't get you sex anymore. I have a theory you might not agree with right away, but I encourage you to think about it awhile.

When you were dating your wife or very early in your marriage, you were doing many of the things that made her feel close to you: spending time with her, listening to her, praising her, responding to her feedback in your life and keeping your word. She already felt close to you. You were already doing all the global connective things that let her put her guard down and desire you.

You may want to focus on who you were in those early days of your relationship if you want to repeat that sexual success now. For those of you still looking for her elusive button, you can continue searching in vain, or you can decide to do the things that made the relational environment warm enough to develop into marriage in the first place.

My personal belief is that women don't have external buttons. I don't think her button exists in a physical location. So, if you have tried to find it there, you may be looking in all the wrong places. If there is a button, I think it is inside of her where she processes her thoughts and feelings—it is her need for security and a close relationship with you.

There are women who don't desire sex for other reasons, including illness, depression or past sexual abuse. They may need professional help for these issues. Some are sexually anorexic and do not want intimacy. Others have lost their desire for sex because of the one-dimensional type of selfish sex that they have received over the years, which has left them feeling empty and lonely.

For the wife who doesn't respond to you positively after sixty days of putting the "oil" in her regularly, it may be time to seek professional help. She may need medical, sexual or psychological help. If a woman has no desire for sex, you can't make her want sex. I have also met men who did not desire sex. The reality is that there are people with issues so great that even the most helpful principles in this book won't work for them without some professional assistance. If you are in a situation like this, get professional help. Until you do, your chances of sexual success are limited.

BAIT AND SWITCH

Many of my male clients complain that their sexual life used to be much better than it is now. Their spouse was great in the beginning of their relationship. They couldn't ask for more. She was exciting and adventurous, and she even initiated sex. They thought that they were the absolute luckiest man in the world. Then everything started to change for the worse.

Now she doesn't want to perform certain sexual behaviors anymore or wear particular clothes. She is not comfortable when he does certain things now. At first the husband acquiesced, but when the situation repeated itself regarding yet another sexual behavior in which they had regularly engaged, he began to be resentful.

These changes continue throughout the marriage, leaving the husband pretty limited and not as adventurous as he once was with her. He no longer complains (because any sex is better than no sex), but he is now beginning to feel anger and contempt because of the changes. She's no longer inviting him to be intimate and rarely talks about sex anymore. In short, his sexual life has deteriorated, and he didn't even get to vote on it.

If you relate to this scenario, it is important that you understand why you feel the way you do. Your spouse made unilateral sexual decisions that affect your sexual expression. You don't want to address it because she has learned to throw you a few lines that paralyze you, such as, "All you want is sex!" or "Aren't you ever satisfied?" So you probably have closed up because you know your sexual supply may be completely cut off otherwise. What happened? This is a description of the very common bait-and-switch syndrome that spouses can get into over the course of their relationship.

Women are not the only ones who can bait and switch in a relationship; men can be guilty, too. Your wife still believes in your initial promise to love her, to be intimate, to make her your first priority, to help with the kids and to talk to her rather than watching television. Now she feels ignored, unimportant and somewhat used within the relationship. She feels cheated as well and resentful about the empty promises you made concerning your relationship. She may feel alone and overly responsible for the children, finances and work. She feels that you baited and then switched.

It's hard to say whose bait and switch came first in your relationship. Both husband and wife can be responsible for this bait-and-switch syndrome in the marriage. Early on in the relationship either spouse can oversell their true interest and sincerity in any area. He may initially convince her of his financial stability, only to start spending impulsively once they are married. He may keep his pornography habit a secret prior to marriage, but his wife discovers it and feels he lied to her. She may oversell how much she wants to have sex before she is faced with the children, a dog, PTA, PMS and financial stress. Or she may actually trap you intentionally for reasons you don't know—financial security, prestige and so forth.

If you need to address this problem, your focus should be on your own areas of bait and switch. After you fix those areas of concern—and only after!—you can examine your spouse's problem areas because then you will have done more than just talk about your weaknesses; you will have changed.

If you feel angry about having to do all of this relational work, you may want to look into the anger exercise that we discussed. (See chapter three.) After we discuss other issues of sexual agreement and building intimacy (chapters ten and eleven), you may find release from your resentments. Remember, sexual success is not automatic, but it is possible to complete the journey and become sexually successful.

SEXUAL PERSONALITIES

We all have sexual personalities that reflect characteristics of our total personality. It is natural for some personalities to enjoy taking risks. They love to explore and are creative. Other personalities are more cautious and conservative. They enjoy the familiar and find security in the comfort of their surroundings.

A man whose overall personality makes him a high achiever and risk taker will bring those qualities into his sexual expression. He will probably want to try different positions or places to engage in sex and will enjoy variety in his expression. These characteristics are an extension of his personality.

Then there is his beautiful, cautious wife, who drives the speed limit, dresses conservatively and always obeys the rules. More than likely she will exhibit this conservatism in her sexual personality as well. She is a great person, but she is not going to behave like her husband in the bedroom because of her overall conservative personality.

Most men are wise enough to marry a stable woman whose personality is a great balance to his. However, many men have dated women with various kinds of personalities that do not match the type of personality they married. For this reason, they may be tempted to try to change their wife to match someone they previously knew.

It is not her fault that you have had experiences in your past with other women, pornography or your fantasies. Why should your wife suffer the consequences of your lustful desires? They are a result of your sin, not your wife's. If you live with a feeling of entitlement that says you should have the sexual experience you desire, you could damage your wife sexually, preventing her from becoming who she could be sexually.

Take a minute to think about your wife's personality outside of the bedroom. Is she a gal who takes uncalculated risks? Does she have lots of ambition for various kinds of accomplishments? Does she try new things just for fun? Does she drive the speed limit? Does she like to follow the rules?

Understanding that your wife's sexual personality is similar to her nonsexual personality can help you to accept her as she is. If you can objectively accept her for who she is instead of who you wish she were, you can at least begin to deal with sexual issues in the light of reality.

Working with your wife toward a mutual sexual agreement involves a process of negotiation that will require you to be realistic about each other's sexual personality. (See chapter eleven.) As you grow in acceptance of each other's sexual persona and begin to negotiate your mutual sexuality, you can find a place of sexual peace with each other. Neither personality should seek to dominate or control the mutual sexual expression of the marriage.

I don't know when it was that I first realized I needed to accept my wife's sexual personality. But when I did, it helped me significantly to know that I didn't need to try to change her. What a relief! That doesn't mean we didn't discuss our sexual preferences with each other. It just helped to take the attitude-type issues out of the process.

HER SEXUAL ESTEEM

Women have experienced their own sexual journey before they met their husband. Some saved themselves for the man they married and may feel insecure about their sexuality. Others have had a variety of sexual experiences that left them with either positive or negative feelings about their sexuality. About one-third of women have experienced sexual abuse as a child or rape as a young adult, which has left inevitable scars. Regardless of your wife's previous sexual journey, her sexual self-esteem issues are now in your hands.

Negative feelings from a lack of self-esteem run very deep and can overcome reason. I've counseled with many unhappy men who are smart, handsome and wealthy and who lead what appears to be a great life. They feel as if they've never measured up. They have never heard a reassuring "good job" from anyone. What they have heard is: "You're stupid." "You won't amount to anything." "Why can't you do things right?" As these messages are repeated over and over, they begin to sink deep within the man's heart and play a huge role in the negative way he sees himself.

The same is true of a woman's sexual self-esteem. Imagine the negative effects on a woman who hears her husband criticize her sexuality: "You're not like you used to be." "Why can't we engage in that behavior more?" "Why have you gained so much weight?" After years of hearing the message that her husband wants more, better and different sex than she gives him, the wife concludes he will never be satisfied with her because she is not good enough. She will never measure up, so why even try? As a result of not feeling accepted, her desire for sex slowly diminishes. This is a natural response to her husband's rejection. Who wants to do something that they're inadequate at?

After reading this, perhaps you see the effects of some negative things that you've done or said to your wife. You may have inadvertently created a situation that did not build her up sexually but instead, actually tore down her sexual self-esteem. Whether she believes she has lost her sexual self-esteem because of your words or because of her past sexual experiences, her attitude toward sex will be negatively affected.

I have heard success defined as the ability to make others feel or become successful. I can't think of a better place to apply this success principle than in the bedroom. If you consistently build up your wife in this area, reassuring her that she's a competent and great lover, you will help build her sexual confidence, which may lead her into a new freedom to take risks and actually enjoy having sex with you. It's up to you. The following stories relate the power you have to help or hurt your wife's sexual esteem

~

Tony had a few sexual encounters before marriage. Then he had a spiritual awakening and began to attend a Christian singles group where he met his wife. His wife, however, grew up in the church and waited until she was married to have sex. She was attractive, healthy and yet felt insecure next to her husband. On their wedding night shortly after they were intimate, she asked him how he felt. He thought he should be honest, so he said, "It was OK, but I've had better."

Needless to say, those words devastated his wife's sexual self-esteem. From that night forward, they had difficulties with sex and sexual frequency that plagued their entire marriage. Because of her lack of sexual self-esteem, she did not desire sex to be a part of their marriage. Tony has lived to regret those thoughtless words he said to her on his wedding night his entire life.

Dennis had sex with many women during his young adult life. Eventually he settled down and decided to marry a nice girl. Like Tony, he fell in love with a church girl who never had sex prior to marriage. On their wedding night he told her that their sexual experience was the best sex he had ever had. He regularly praised his wife during their sexual experiences. He not only praised her in the bedroom, but outside of the bedroom as well. He intentionally and consistently built up her sexual self-esteem.

Over the course of Dennis's marriage, sex has never been a negative issue. His wife enjoys sex and feels rather good about herself and about their sexual life together. She has a quiet sexual confidence that comes from believing she is a great lover and that she pleases her husband.

Obviously we can all learn from each other's mistakes and successes. The point is to be aware of your wife's need for sexual self-esteem and take responsibility to build that in her. This is vital for your ultimate sexual success. If you pour good into her, over time good will flow back to you. Remember the biblical principle: "You reap what you sow." This principle also applies in the holy of holies—your bedroom.

THREE KEY WORDS

In all the years I've counseled adults about sexual issues, I have never heard anyone articulate the importance of *words* during sex. Words are crucial to sexual success! As we discussed earlier, you and your spouse both are absolutely the most vulnerable that you can be while having sex. What you say or don't say to your wife when you are together sexually communicates to the core of her being.

The more aware you are that sex is a three-dimensional act involving spirit, soul and body, the more you will realize how important your words are to your wife. If you can only talk in object-type terms to her, you will communicate to your wife that body sex (one-dimensional) is all you want. If you ignore the mind and emotions of your spouse during sex, you are sending the powerful message that her body is important to you; her person is not.

There are three key words that women yearn to hear during sex, yet most women never hear them. My clients who have learned to use these three words have found out just how powerful they are. I can tell you how countless women burst into tears of joy when they heard them because they thought they would never hear them from their husbands.

The three key words are not "I love you"; they are "You satisfy me." This simple but profound expression spoken sincerely by you can do wonders for your wife's sexual self-esteem. She longs to know that she sexually satisfies her husband. The fact that you can even admit that you are "totally pleased" with her person and her sexual expression, that you don't need more, different or better sex, can relieve her of a terrible burden to measure up.

Her deep yearning to know she satisfies you is much like the ache many men have in their hearts to hear their dad say "I love you" or "I'm proud of you, son." Hearing the words that you long to hear can change your life. For many women, that change can be dramatic.

Look her right in the eye when you say, "You satisfy me." Tell her she's a great lover. Acknowledging that you actually can be satisfied will bring a real sense of peace to your wife. I encourage you to try saying these words to her as a regular part of your lovemaking. Over time she will come to believe these words are right from your heart.

These three words not only have tremendous power when spoken sincerely during times of intimacy when you can plant them deep into her spirit and soul; they are also powerful when spoken to her outside the bedroom. During a casual conversation with your wife remind her of how she satisfies you sexually. A day or two after being sexual, look her in the eye and tell her that she really satisfied you sexually. Say something like, "You know, I still feel so satisfied from our lovemaking the other day." You can even take it a step further. While sitting on a sofa together say to her, "You know, I was thinking about making love to you today, but I am still so satisfied from the last time I think I'm going to wait."

Let me warn you, this kind of praise will stir your wife. Conveying to her that you thought about having sex but concluded you were still satisfied, instead of groping and hassling her for more, will astound her. She won't even know how to respond to this totally new encounter with her husband.

As you continue to praise her in this way, you will begin to see her sexual self-esteem grow. As it does, she will begin to relax sexually. Most women feel as if they are the bone and you are the hungry dog. They expect that at any minute you are going to lunge at them. When a wife clearly gets these three words into her spirit and soul that her husband is satisfied with her, new frontiers of sexual success can open for her and for you.

An important principle for being sexually successful involves building your wife's confidence by complimenting her rather than criticizing her. And you will feel successful because you are adding to her sexual self-esteem. When your wife feels good about sex, you can both begin to enjoy better, more intimate sex.

NINE

Roadblocks to Intimacy

As we continue our journey toward sexual success, we must address a major roadblock that will prevent it—the lack of intimacy. There is a relational dynamic that I have watched repeatedly sabotage couples' intimacy. I call this dynamic "emotional-based relationships." A marriage characterized as an emotional-based relationship fails to establish principles by which husband and wife make decisions and according to which they live their daily lives.

The sixties' culture produced a generation that bought into a lifestyle based on the philosophy "If it feels good, do it." Concepts of restraint, principles and accountability so vital to a successful marriage in every area are not a part of the decision-making process for people in emotional-based relationships. Instead, this marriage is characterized by chaos, lack of follow-through and multiple inconsistencies in several areas of the marriage, including the disciplines in raising children.

BENIGN EMOTIONAL-BASED RELATIONSHIPS

There are two types of emotional-based relationships. The first is what I call the "benign" form. In this syndrome neither the husband nor the wife is intentionally trying to be difficult. Neither spouse desires harm for the other; they simply can't seem to "get it together."

A couple I've known for several years fits this description. They are raising two children and are always so busy that it is difficult for them to have time for each other. They have no time for intimacy or dating. Their house is always a mess, with piles of clothes everywhere; there is very little order in their lives. Other areas of their life such as finances are also in total chaos.

They tried therapy for their sexual problems, but typically didn't continue doing their homework for very long. When asked why they didn't follow through, they rarely can give a tangible reason. The entire notion of practiced consistency or principle-based thinking eludes them. They make their decisions based on their emotions, and their schedules change continually simply because of their current desire to do something else. As a result, they are unable to remember previous commitments and repeatedly miss events they had planned to attend. Though they mean no one harm and are often pleasant and fun to be around, there is no structure in their lives to help them be successful.

Improving their sexual relationship comes slowly to a marriage functioning in the benign form of this emotional-based relationship system. Trying to get them to commit to any discipline necessary for a sense of connecting is difficult. When they do manage to follow guidelines for improving intimacy for a few weeks, they feel closer than ever. But they discontinue the system shortly, and their relationship deteriorates again.

The reason for the deterioration is that this couple's emotions dominate the decision-making process. As we have stated, if they feel like doing something, they do it; if they don't feel like doing it (even if it is the right thing to do), they just don't do it. They are unable to apply principles for successful sexuality to their lives on a consistent basis.

This type of emotional-based system plays havoc with intimacy and sex because intimacy building happens as a result of a lifestyle of discipline practiced over a lifetime. Successful sexuality can be described as relational wealth that accumulates through a lifelong investment of consistent behavior. Like material wealth, relational wealth—intimacy—doesn't just happen. It is painstakingly achieved by choosing to complete a journey along a pathway where two hearts are consistently available and open to each other.

MALIGNANT EMOTIONAL-BASED RELATIONSHIPS

The malignant form of the emotional-based relationship is rooted in rebellion or willfulness. In this dysfunctional marriage, not only are the husband and wife making their decisions based on their changing emotions, but they also refuse instruction, advice or relational accountability to anyone. They are bent on doing what they want at the moment, regardless of the results. If they want to neglect their spouse for days or weeks in order to punish them, they will. If they want to make a financial decision without considering the consequences, they will.

This kind of selfishness that does not consider others becomes toxic in any relationship, and especially in marriage. Intimacy experienced by couples in this kind of relationship is at best inconsistent and at worst, volatile. Anger or silence is often used to control the spouse and other family members as well. One characteristic of a malignant relationship is when the major goal of the family is to keep one spouse happy.

This malignant form of an emotional-based marriage can sometimes be a result of an emotional disorder that is undiagnosed in one spouse. In other marriages, addictions can cause this unhappy syndrome. A spouse may be addicted to work, alcohol, drugs or sex. Findings in medical literature support the fact that addiction of any kind reflects emotional immaturity.

Another cause of this malignant syndrome is the mood disorder known as bipolar disorder. This biological brain chemistry issue affects even stable marriages. The spouse suffering from bipolar disorder has days of happy, motivated, clear thinking, and is actually fun to be around. Then seemingly out of the blue, the troubled spouse becomes moody and unreasonably irritable for several days. During these dark days no one in the family can do anything right, and family members feel a "why bother" attitude creep into the atmosphere of the home. After a couple of days, the moody spouse becomes happy again, and life gets back to normal. This cycle of moodiness, which can occur weekly, can keep a marriage in chaos regularly.

Successful sexuality can be described as relational wealth that accumulates through a lifelong investment of consistent behavior.

A relationship that fits this malignant description but is not a result of an emotional disorder or addiction may be caused by the rebellious attitude that declares, "I will do what I want, and if you don't like it, you can leave." The rebellious spouse in this relationship often makes the other spouse seem needy or weak if they express desire or need for intimacy. The one desiring intimacy feels as if their spouse can't or won't let them in.

If you feel that you are in a malignant or toxic emotional-based relationship, you may need to seek further professional help to work through the problem with your spouse so you can be more sexually successful. Real problems need to be addressed in real ways professionally. In the meantime, I suggest you try to utilize as many of the exercises presented in this book as you can to see if you experience some improvement.

IMMATURITY IN EMOTIONAL-BASED RELATIONSHIPS

These emotional-based relationships we have described also evolve because one or both spouses behave as a child or adolescent in a major area of their adult life. Men and women can be an adult in one area of life while still acting as an adolescent or child in other areas. This immaturity creates imbalances in the marriage relationship that can result in emotional-based systems that make sexual success difficult. Maturity of both spouses is required, as we will discuss, for healthy, principle-based relationships.

Jerry and Paula struggled with emotional immaturity in their relationship. Jerry was a great salesman in a local business who walked in personal integrity. Socially, Jerry's friends would also agree that Jerry functioned as a mature adult. He was also an adult when it came to recreational fun with friends and business associates, planning time for them to fish, hunt and attend sporting events together.

However, in the area of personal finances Jerry behaved like a child. He didn't know what came in or even what went out of the checkbook. He would only engage in the financial process for his personal needs and to sign his tax returns. His wife, Paula, handled all the financial decisions and accounting of them. Even though Jerry was an adult concerning social activities and fun, he lacked adult skills and development in this important area of finances.

Jerry reacted emotionally instead of responsibly to financial pressures, which placed undue stress on his relationship with Paula. She didn't like handling all of the finances and was overwhelmed with Jerry's immature approach to life in this area. His inability to be responsible in this area placed strain in their marriage relationship that limited their intimacy. However, the pressure this issue brought into their marriage was not Jerry's fault alone.

Paula, though a sweet person in many ways, had some areas of immaturity in her life as well. She was an adult when it came to the social, financial and spiritual areas of her life. But in the area of sexuality, she was a child. She took no sexual responsibility in the relationship. Neither Jerry nor Paula could remember one time that Paula initiated sex.

Although Paula was a perfect wife and mother, she couldn't express feelings of intimacy. She had difficulty practicing the feelings exercise (see chapter ten), and she resisted letting anyone get to know her emotionally. This immature behavior added strain to the marriage, and especially to their sexual intimacy. These areas of immaturity in Jerry and Paula created an unhealthy emotional-based system. To people around them their lives looked OK, but inside their home there was a quiet, steady resentment building.

Many couples can relate their experience to that of Jerry and Paula. They can identify areas of responsibility that were not comfortable for them as they grew up. Consciously or unconsciously, they kept hoping that the person they married would handle these uncomfortable areas for them. Often the problem is never communicated with the spouse; it just presents itself in living life. Then the emotional systems for decision making evolve, causing negative feelings that create a roadblock to intimacy.

As a result, sexual success becomes difficult. If both spouses are not functioning as adults within their relationship, their areas of immaturity will rob them of intimacy.

These issues of irresponsibility will determine how sexually successful a couple can become.

The more adult you become in every area of your life, the safer your wife will feel and the more respect and honor she will have for you. When you act like a child or an adolescent, your wife will feel like your mother, not your lover. She knows when you are being irresponsible in an area of your life. As someone has said, "If you don't want your wife to act like your mother, stop acting like a child."

Any couple living in an emotional-based relationship that is not established on sound principles for relationship will find it difficult to change the relationship. Even the benign form of emotional-based relationships resists the disciplines required to bring change. The daily chaos within this system distracts the couple from the effort required to bring structure and consistency into the relationship.

Crises are created by the lack of discipline in their lives, resulting in the needs of one or both spouses going unmet and causing further stress in the relationship. Something as simple as a flat tire or an unwillingness to discuss future plans can trigger another round of chaos . . . and the cycle of the emotional-based marriage starts over once again.

As we have discussed, these emotional-based relationships, whether benign or malignant, can create a major roadblock to sex and intimacy! If you are unsure if your marriage falls into this category, the questions below will help you to identify your situation.

NOTE: This understanding can only be used to identify your own areas of immaturity where personal growth is needed. Remember, you *cannot* change your spouse; that is impossible. So unless you use this information for individual development, in a therapeutic manner, it can become less than productive. Please don't use this information to attack, shame or otherwise injure the soul of your spouse. It is meant to help you in a therapeutic manner for your self-development.

Be as honest and thoughtful as you can when you answer the following questions. Answering *yes* to several of these questions may mean that your marriage fits the description of an emotional-based system.

1. Does your marriage and family life feel chaotic most of the time? ❑ Yes ❑ No

2. Does it feel as if there is no consistent spiritual and emotional connection with your spouse? ❑ Yes ❑ No

3. Does money get spent regularly without anyone really knowing where it all goes? ❑ Yes ❑ No

4. Does it appear that you don't have long-term retirement plans you're working toward? ❑ Yes ❑ No

5. Does it seem that some things never get done? ❑ Yes ❑ No

6. Does it seem unclear how decisions get made within the relationship or marriage? ❑ Yes ❑ No

PRINCIPLE-BASED RELATIONSHIPS

The opposite of an emotional-based relationship is a relationship committed to principles. Principles that have been agreed to between spouses guide the decision-making process in the relationship, overruling their more unpredictable emotions. One spouse's personality doesn't dominate or force his or her desires on the other person in the relationship.

A couple who lives in a principle-based relationship works together to solve problems. They don't live just to serve their emotions. If they don't feel like doing something they committed to do, their commitment to principle overrules their self-discomfort and helps them complete what they agreed to do.

Couples committed to a principle-based relationship have the greatest chance of achieving and maintaining a life-long intimate relationship that benefits both spouses and brings them to the goal of successful sexuality. In principle-based marriages intimacy can flourish over time and sex becomes easier to negotiate. These marriages create strong, safe systems that help couples to connect intimately and stay connected for the rest of their lives. The husband who establishes his marriage on consistent principles is going to have a happy sexual wife for a very long time.

The good news is that couples who are presently living in an emotional-based system can move into a more principle-based system. The exercises and structures discussed in later chapters that can move a couple toward a principle-based relationship will require a determined effort from both spouses in order to overrule the habits of their emotional responses. They will need to move beyond the "if it feels good, do it" philosophy that has created their unhealthy emotional-based relationship. I strongly encourage you as men to commit to the work required to overcome any present difficulties and move toward sexual success.

A couple who lives in a principle-based relationship works together to solve problems.

Intimacy is not acquired by the lazy, fainthearted or undisciplined; it is achieved by taking the challenge to make it a lifelong goal. Intimacy is a fruit that is produced by becoming consistent in cultivating behaviors in a marriage relationship that result in sexual success. (See following chapters for these specific behaviors.)

EVALUATING YOUR MATURITY LEVELS

Referring to the following chart will help you to evaluate your personal maturity levels at present in the areas listed.

Area	Child	Adolescent	Adult
Spiritual	Refuses to feed themselves by reading the Bible or other spiritual books	Feeds self with spiritual material	Feeds self regularly
	Wants others to feed them only by attending church or religious meeting	Their interpretation of spirituality is "the" interpretation	Feeds others in their life by character and word
	Prayer is not really initiated on a regular basis	Prays but is inconsistent	Prayer is consistent and desired
	Likes it if "you" pray	Will pray together "if you make them"	Desires to pray with you anytime
	States that the Bible or religion is too difficult to understand	Struggles with balancing truth and their behavior	
	Doesn't feel convicted of wrong on any regular basis	Convicted of wrong sometimes but has struggles with authority issues	Convicted of wrong, even smaller behaviors regularly
Social	Does not initiate in relationships	Will initiate in relationship if it serves a purpose	Can initiate a relationship just because, with no need to serve a purpose
	Only responds to those who want to initiate toward them	Relationship based on activities	Can create time just for relating not requiring an activity
	Can't seem to find a person or group to connect to	Tends to have a rotating best friend	Can have long-term friendships
	Their friends do all the work in their relationships	Does some initiating in the relationship to set up activities	Accepts the seasons of friendships
			Tends to initiate equally in a relationship

Area	Child	Adolescent	Adult
Financial	Refuses to have anything to do with money issues	Financially selfish	Money has spiritual meaning
	Money things are just overwhelming	Thinks in short-term, materialistic tendencies	Long-term planning is part of their thought process
	Has a naive status toward taxes and retirement	Toys are more important than future planning	Short-term sacrifice is honorable for long term gain
	As long as their needs are met there is no real need to talk about it	What they are, the family looks like (house, cars, clothes) is really important	
	Doesn't write checks or know the bills	Credit card debt is very common	Tithing is consistent
		Will tithe when convenient	
Sexual	Does not accept or see themselves as sexual	Sex is for them mostly	Accepts themselves sexually
	Will not initiate sex	Unaware of spouse's sexual needs	Accepts the sexuality of their spouse
		Angry when their needs don't get met	Has intimacy during sexuality
	Talking about sex is always inappropriate	Sex conversations seem to feel cheap and not about intimacy	Maintains sexual integrity
Feelings	Doesn't know what you're talking about	Has feelings but limited ability to communicate them	Has learned how to identify and communicate feelings
	Becomes confused when emotions addressed	Has periods of emotional constipation, then blows up or gets silent	Can be emotionally safe and keep confidences
	Feels you're asking too much of them to do feeling work	Really more concerned about their feelings and not yours	Values and hears the feelings of their spouses

Area	Child	Adolescent	Adult
Fun	Can have some fun if others plan for it	Fun is what life is about	Can plan fun for self and others
	Loves to be invited but has little fun on their own	Keeps self preoccupied by several hobbies	Realizes the importance of fun in balance
	Often unable to be silly at appropriate times	Selfish with their time off and on vacation	Will take some time for self but balances it with their spouse
		Most of their friends revolve around hobbies	

In the columns below you can indicate where you believe you may fit in the above categories: child, adolescent or adult. If you feel more comfortable writing your answers on a separate sheet of paper, feel free to do that. Remember to score yourself only. I know you can't help but score your spouse, but if you do, don't tell them. They may disagree.

Area	Child	Adolescent	Adult
Spiritual			
Social			
Financial			
Sexual			
Feelings			
Fun			

These issues listed are emotionally based and often represent the hot buttons within a marriage. To resolve these issues will require individual work, not couple work. The couple work comes in to play when you move beyond these issues and can discuss them with each other and see the impact that your development in an area is making on the relationship.

Your reaction at this point may be, *I thought we were talking about sex*. Let me assure you; we *are* talking about sex. The less stress and chaos these issues cause in a relationship, the more likely you will feel close to each other. When you feel close to each other regularly, *whammo*, you're having more sex. If your lives are consistently chaotic and you are constantly angry at each other, you're too mad to have sex and are probably sleeping on the proverbial sofa. It's hard to have sexual success when you're in a different room of the house than your spouse. The better the quality of your relationship in everyday living, the more likely you are to have sexual success.

If you are willing to grow and develop into an adult in areas that you identified yourself as a child or adolescent, your journey toward successful sexuality can take you to a wonderful end. As you learn to apply the principles we will discuss in the following chapters, you will remove other roadblocks that may be hindering the intimacy you and your spouse desire. This will make your sexual success much easier to obtain.

I have counseled several couples who had no sexual relationship for over ten years. After six to eight weeks of following the principles in the next chapter, they not only were having regular sex, but they also liked each other again. Principles when followed can bring new life to a relationship. Then sexual success is right around the corner.

TEN

"Three a Day" for Intimacy

hrough my years of counseling Christian couples, one thing I have learned is that many marriages have little to no structure that encourages intimacy in their relationship. The lack of prioritizing relational closeness to each other and neglecting to develop intimacy skills in the relationship can limit future sexual success even for Christian couples. Too many people grow up believing they will get married and live happily ever after. Yet they are often not equipped with knowledge that will encourage the building of intimacy in their marriage for a lifetime of satisfaction. They are disappointed when they discover that their spouse doesn't know the secret code to intimacy either.

In the early months or years of marriage, couples have fun together as they begin to learn about their spouse, go to work or attend school, get their first apartment and pick out furniture. They attend church and social events and enjoy physical intimacy together without a sense of guilt. The sheer complexities of their new life together along with the multitude of decisions to be made can keep couples talking and sharing with each other regularly.

Then slowly and subtly it happens—no one really knows when or how—but the relationship changes, and the couple doesn't seem to talk as much as they did. Making decisions is not as exciting as when they were first married. Major purchases are fewer, and life and sex begin to take on a certain dull sense of routine. The couple doesn't seem as close to each other; they are just living together. What happened? How did their passion for each other disappear?

A CLASSIC STORY

Roger and Constance are a classic example of a Christian couple who lost their passion for each other. They are both intelligent and successful people. Constance owns a small business, and Roger manages a large organization. They both love God and attend a large healthy church. To know either of them is to love them; they have great personalities. But they share one little secret that no one else knows—not even their pastor, whom they consider their good friend. Roger and Constance don't have sex; they haven't been intimate for six years.

Life priorities change, and there is no longer a structure in the relationship to encourage intimacy.

"What happened to us?" was their question for me as they told me their story. Constance shared with me the history of their relationship. They dated for two years before marrying. During those two years Roger called Constance frequently and wrote her notes that included verses of Scripture. They prayed together and seemed to everyone else to be inseparable friends. After they first married, their sex life was good, fun and frequent. They traveled and did lots of fun things together.

Then after the children came, things changed. Their schedules took them in separate directions, and Roger traveled more. They prayed less frequently together. Soon even talking was minimal, and sex just happened. The fun that had been in their sex life in the beginning of the marriage had disappeared. After the children started to school, Constance started her business, and she and Roger seemed to drift even further apart. Their interests had changed, and most of their conversations were limited to household management issues.

Though Roy and Constance attended church every Sunday, their spiritual life revolved around religion rather than reality of relationship with God and each other. Personal communication finally ceased altogether. Roger read his financial and sports magazines, and Constance was so busy she didn't have the energy to keep the marriage going along with her other activities.

Occasionally they reassured each other of their mutual love and would sometimes talk about sex—but neither one followed through. Intimacy had been somehow squeezed out of their relationship, and neither spouse knew why. When Constance finished sharing, I asked Roger if her perspective of the relationship history was accurate. He concurred that it was.

This couple's story of losing the passion in their marriage is repeated in many marriages. The reason? Life priorities change, and there is no longer a structure in the relationship to encourage intimacy. Passion in marriage is a result of making intimacy a priority for life. Many Christian couples think passion either is a part of their relationship, or it isn't. The truth is that passion is a dividend that comes from making consistent investments in the priorities of a marriage relationship.

REMEMBER YOUR BEGINNINGS

Think about the beginning of your relationship with your wife when you were dating and trying to sell her on the idea that being married to you would be a good idea. Do you remember the passion that you felt for the girl you wanted to marry? Of course you do. What you may not have realized is that the basis of that passion was founded on the priority that relationship had in your life.

Do you remember how you "made" time to be with her? You planned your days and weeks around each other's work schedule, including your days off. Those of you who, like me, moved away from a future spouse to go to school probably had phone bills that proved the priority of that relationship. Those phone bills took a large portion of the little income I made. But it was worth it just to tell her about my day.

Do you remember how spiritual you were? You prayed individually and together as often as you could. You may even have read the Bible together. You were motivated to pray by a strong desire to know God's will and because you needed God to help you stay pure while expressing your love to each other.

Do you remember the gratitude you had for the smallest things your spouse did for you? This was especially true for me when my future spouse cooked for me. I was so grateful! You probably offered a constant stream of praise for everything this special person did. Do you remember when you thought she was so smart and attractive and that she had so much potential? You believed in her and regularly encouraged her.

The passion you felt was a result of making this relationship your priority in life. Many couples try to get the passion back into their relationship, when what they need to do is to get their priorities back. Once you reestablish the priority of the relationship, the passion naturally follows and grows.

A HEALING STRUCTURE

Many couples who come to me for help to restore their marriage to health are suffering from sprains or fractures in the structure of their relationship. These injuries are as real to a marriage as a broken leg is to a physical body. To continue the analogy, when a leg is broken, the patient makes an appointment with a doctor or goes to the emergency room to get it fixed.

> Many couples try to get the passion back into their relationship, when what they need to do is to get their priorities back.

The first thing the doctor does is x-ray the leg; that's right, he is examining the structure. If the leg is broken, the x-ray shows a damaged structure—the bone. The treatment the doctor usually applies to this structural damage is a cast to hold the bone in place while it heals. The cast is a temporary structure that will aid the healing of the permanent structure. The cast is made of plastic or plaster and has no innate healing properties. But when it is applied to a broken bone by a skilled physician—surprise! Healing of the bone can and does happen.

Working to regain priorities in a marriage can act like a "cast" that will allow brokenness to mend. No matter how strained or broken the relationship, healing can and does take place when proper structures are used to help the healing process. I encourage all couples suffering in an emotional-based system to apply a "cast" of principles to their brokenness to initiate the healing process. And I have seen literal miracles of restored marriages result when couples decide to put priorities back into their relationship.

THE THREE DAILIES

One of the priority structures I apply to broken marriage relationships I call *the three dailies*. When Roger and Constance restored their priority structure by practicing the three dailies in their relationship, they admitted that it was hard work at first. But over time it became easier, and now these priority structures are just part of their routine.

Roger and Constance are doing much better since they incorporated the three dailies into their life. Not only are they still in love, but they are more in love with each other than ever before. Roger even joked about how he likes Constance a whole lot more now. And Constance says, "I feel like I know his heart now and feel really special and close to him."

"So what about the sex?" I ask.

They both laugh and affirm that not only is it very consistent, but also it's more fun and fulfilling than when they were younger. I give Roger a high five, laughing with them. What can I say? I love my job!

DAILY #1—PRAYER

Prayer is an absolutely necessary part of the healing structure that you need to practice daily with your spouse. I am constantly amazed when Christian couples tell me that the last time they prayed together (not including blessing the food or a good-night prayer with children) was years ago. Usually their rationale for neglecting this effort goes something like, "We both pray, just not together."

It's good that spouses pray individually, but that is not the optimal pattern for building intimacy in a marriage. Psalm 127:1 says, "Unless the LORD builds the house, its builders labor in vain." This verse shows the importance of involving the Lord in the building process of your house. It will keep you from futile labors that are doomed to fail. Prayer is an active way to make the Lord be a part of the building of your marriage.

Matthew 18:19 underlines the importance of two people agreeing in prayer: "Again, I tell you that if two of you on earth agree about anything you ask for, it will be done for you by my Father in heaven." Two people are required to qualify for the promise of this prayer of agreement; it doesn't happen when one person prays.

To understand the overall importance of prayer, consider the role of Christ Himself who is seated in the heavens since His resurrection from the dead. Scripture declares, "Christ Jesus, who died—more than that, who was raised to life—is at the right hand of God and is also interceding for us" (Rom. 8:34). The Lord Jesus is praying for us continually. Those who have learned to intercede actively in prayer know that God's pleasure is to commune with us through prayer, not just individually, but as a couple as well.

Men, it is your responsibility as head of your home to be a spiritual guide for your wife and pray with her. When you go to work, your boss communicates to you what the responsibilities of your job are. I have rarely met anyone who liked every part of his job. You may complain, but you have to get over it and do it anyway. The bottom line is, you do the job.

The Bible teaches that anyone who knows the good he ought to do and doesn't do it sins (James 4:17). A Christian man who knows what the Bible teaches about prayer and yet doesn't lead his wife in prayer is sinning. He is hurting the marriage relationship through his neglect of this biblical structure.

We serve a holy God, and I believe He will hold us accountable to give Him a good return on His investment He left with us. He gave each of us one of His precious daughters to be a wife. She is like the talent the landowner gave to his servant in the parable Jesus told:

Again, it will be like a man going on a journey, who

called his servants and entrusted his property to them. To one he gave five talents of money, to another two talents, and to another one talent, each according to his ability. Then he went on his journey. The man who had received the five talents went at once and put his money to work and gained five more. So also, the one with the two talents gained two more. But the man who had received the one talent went off, dug a hole in the ground and hid his master's money.

After a long time the master of those servants returned and settled accounts with them. The man who had received the five talents brought the other five. "Master," he said, "you entrusted me with five talents. See, I have gained five more."

His master replied, "Well done, good and faithful servant! You have been faithful with a few things; I will put you in charge of many things. Come and share your master's happiness!"

The man with the two talents also came. "Master," he said, "you entrusted me with two talents; see, I have gained two more."

His master replied, "Well done, good and faithful servant! You have been faithful with a few things; I will put you in charge of many things. Come and share your master's happiness!"

Then the man who had received the one talent came. "Master," he said, "I knew that you are a hard man, harvesting where you have not sown and gathering where you have not scattered seed. So I was afraid and went out and hid your talent in the ground. See, here is what belongs to you."

His master replied, "You wicked, lazy servant! So you knew that I harvest where I have not sown and gather where I have not scattered seed? Well then, you should have put my money on deposit with the bankers, so that when I returned I would have received it back with interest.

"Take the talent from him and give it to the one who has the ten talents. For everyone who has will be given more, and he will have an abundance. Whoever does not have, even what he has will be taken from him. And throw that worthless servant outside, into the darkness, where there will be weeping and gnashing of teeth."

—MATTHEW 25:14–30

The minimal return that the master expected from the man with one talent regardless of his fears, insecurities or his poor view of his master was earned interest. The master was not happy with this wicked servant who neglected to make any effort to increase his investment. Of course, a talent literally represented a sum of money. As a man, you can appreciate the value of money and the need to make a good investment with it. As an analogy, the talent can represent anything of value for which we are asked to be responsible.

If you are a father, let me ask you about the value you place on your little girl—your daughter. You were there when she was born; you played with her, changed her diapers and saw her take her first steps. Remember her very first word? "Da, Da." You gave her all you could: clothes, money for hundreds of things you thought she wanted, your time, your love, and more importantly, you invested yourself in her. She is by far one of the most valuable persons in your life. Maybe you can appreciate how God values His daughters whom He has given to us as our wives.

As a father, would you be more angry with a man who didn't make any money for your investment with him or with a man who married your daughter saying he was a Christian, but later proved to be so selfish he doesn't even pray with her? I can tell you as a dad that I would be a lot angrier with the man who lied to me about being a Christian and is defrauding my little girl than with one who made a poor investment of my money.

Remember that God is also a Father. He not only created your wife, but He also took special time and creativity to make her just right to be your wife. If she is a Christian, He lives in her by His Spirit; they are one.

I cannot communicate strongly enough the wrath I would have toward the man who defrauded my little girl and me. I believe that God, as a loving heavenly Father of your wife, would experience such wrath toward you if you are lazy and irresponsible on the job of spiritually leading your wife. You will have no excuses to offer when you meet your heavenly Father one day. He will require a reckoning of your investment in His daughter.

Prayer is one of the priorities that must be set in place by a man wanting to be sexually successful.

I want that judgment day to be a blessing to you. I want you to be able to say, "Lord, I received Your daughter as Your investment when she was young and insecure about herself. I built her up through prayer and invested the spiritual life You gave to me in her. Now look at her. She is so much more mature and beautiful than when I received her." If a husband will take his responsibility seriously for allowing the Lord to build his house through prayer, He will enjoy the smile of God on His investment now and for eternity.

Prayer is one of the priorities that must be set in place by a man wanting to be sexually successful. Remember that prayer is just talking aloud to God with your wife in the same way you would talk with a friend. Prayer doesn't have to last for hours. It doesn't require you to kneel or take any other particular posture. It is simply the principle of connecting with God together, and it is essential.

We have learned that intimacy is tri-dimensional, involving spirit, soul and body. As we grow spiritually together, our intimacy in the other two areas will grow as well. I love walking in the garden of my life with my wife, Lisa, and bringing her into the presence of our loving Father in prayer. I really believe this "#1 Daily" has been instrumental in developing the strength and intimacy of our marriage.

DAILY #2—FEELINGS

Communicating emotional responses and learning to honestly share feelings is a second very important skill that spouses need to develop and maintain throughout marriage to be sexually successful. Emotions involve a large part of the soul, along with the intellect and the will. They are an important part of who you and your spouse are. Emotional responses are involved in the way she processes her life events all day long.

Often early in the dating relationship, and even after marriage, couples readily share with each other their feelings about their dreams, life situations, people and even God. After marriage, life gets more complicated and conversations between spouses become more centered on managing who does what and what needs to be paid and the logistics of handling the children.

Marriages can be managed efficiently and function well, and yet spouses lose the connectedness they once had. Eventually they begin to feel alone, unsupported and not understood; they wonder why they are even going through the motions. These same couples tell me they don't know what happened to their feelings after they were married awhile; it seems as if they went into hiding. These feelings are often common with spouses who have not developed a communication system in their marriage for expressing their emotional responses.

Many spouses don't see each other for eight to ten hours of the day. Both have been involved in the big, bad world. People or situations have positively or negatively affected their emotions all day long. Though spouses may be intuitive when talking to their children, wanting to know how the events of their day affected them, they barely get the facts about each other's day, let alone the feelings their spouse experienced.

When I talk with husbands about this need to express their feelings, it is often apparent that they have limited skills in this area. The problem is not that they don't have feelings. Every person comes complete with many feelings as standard operating equipment from their Maker. The problem is the limited skill they have to express them.

I can deeply empathize with these men. I was emotionally illiterate when I got married. Though I had lots of feelings, my childhood background had not offered me opportunity to develop skills to identify or communicate my deep feelings to my beautiful bride, Lisa. In my home, the feelings expressed were three: mad, really mad and other, which just meant slamming a door and leaving.

Even though I had hundreds of feelings, I had only learned these three doors of communicating them. So if I was feeling insignificant, the only way I knew to express that feeling was to get mad, madder or other. That was not expressing the real feeling, but it was the only emotional response I had learned. I'm sure you have been in situations where the emotional response of a person didn't line up with the real feelings the person was having.

Even after completing a master's degree in marriage and family counseling, I still had not been taught skill development in identifying feelings or communicating them. I continued studying this vital area of how to develop skills to express properly feelings and emotions in marriage. I began to realize that most of life is about learning skills.

For example, as a youth, I did not develop mechanical skills to be able to repair cars. So as an adult, just having to lift the hood of a car brings a sense of shame to me. No matter how many degrees or licenses I have in other areas,

I still have no mechanical skills for fixing cars. I am certain that if I take a course in basic mechanics to develop these skills, I could learn what I needed to fix a car.

The same is true when it comes to identifying and communicating feelings; it simply requires training or developing a skill. Instead of feeling shame for not having developed skills in sharing your emotional responses, you can determine to develop the skills necessary to do so.

> For men who lack the skill
> to share their feelings with
> their spouse, it is one of the
> greatest hindrances to having
> healthy intimacy in their marriage.

These skills can be learned by anyone, including men! I can personally testify to being able to develop the skills of communicating my feelings in ways other than what I was taught as a child. And I have witnessed many couples who have grown in the skill of identifying and communicating their feelings to each other with wonderful results.

I could share countless memories of couples taking their first stab at practicing the feelings exercise I asked them to do (included later in this chapter). As they develop their skill, slowly at first, sharing one or two feelings cautiously, their daily commitment to share their true feelings with one another becomes easier. Within one hundred days these couples are sharing their feelings with each other and with me candidly. By practicing together daily they develop the skill to share their feelings, which is critical for intimacy and ultimate sexual success. I have seen husbands and wives move from emotional illiteracy to emotional communicative competence by diligently practicing this exercise.

For men who lack the skill to share their feelings with their spouse, it is one of the greatest hindrances to having healthy intimacy in their marriage. Men who can't share the feelings in their heart because of a lack of training cannot expect heart-to-heart intimacy.

That is why the feelings exercise is critical. Let me warn you that it is an exercise, which means it does require some effort to achieve a degree of mastery. At first, it feels unfamiliar and awkward, much as you may have felt when you started learning to use a computer. With practice the learning curve for that new computer program becomes less, and before you know it, you have it figured out and begin to gain confidence. After awhile, you ask yourself how did you ever live without your wonderful computer.

Life is funny that way; some of the best things in life require some effort to achieve. The effort to restore intimacy to your marriage is worth it when you stop to think what the results could be. Wouldn't it be a great day indeed to know in your heart of hearts that you are completely heard by your spouse and accepted? This kind of warm fuzzy only comes after time and practice to develop the skill of expressing your feelings.

Some people may think they can enjoy a mountain view without climbing up the mountains. Living in Colorado, I know firsthand that the climb is as much a part of the fun as the view at the end of the climb. The following exercise is part of the climb to restored intimacy in your marriage. It is designed to help you develop the skill you need to share your feelings with the wonderful woman you married. Whatever difficulties you encounter during the "climb" will be worth it when you achieve the desired results of sexual success.

The Feelings Exercise

The feelings exercise is relatively simple. Choose a feeling from the list of feelings in Appendix B. Then use the feeling word you chose in the following two sentences:

1.   I feel _____ (feeling word) when
     _____.

2.   I first remember feeling _____
     (same feeling word) when _____.

Example 1:

1.   I feel **adventurous** when **I take my two children hiking up the mountains in Colorado Springs.**

2.   I first remember feeling **adventurous** when **I was about thirteen years old and my mom bought me a ten-speed bike that I rode all over town.**

Example 2:

1.   I feel **calm** when **I can get alone in nature and sit really still for a short while.**

2.   I first remember feeling **calm** when **I was first taken out of foster homes and my mom gave me a stuffed animal that I could sleep with.**

In the first sentence you choose whatever feeling you want and give a present-tense example of the feeling. In the second sentence you use the same feeling word, but you choose an early experience from childhood or adolescence that it relates to.

It is the feeling from the past that can be difficult to remember. Do not cop out and try to give an example from a year or so ago. Think hard and do the exercise correctly. Some people who have difficulty trying to remember a situation from the past that relates to a certain feeling have found it easier to begin with a feeling they do remember from a situation in their childhood. They can then use that feeling word in a present-tense situation also.

For example, someone might remember a childhood experience where their mother or father forgot to pick them up from school one day. One of the feelings they might describe is *aloneness* because everyone else had gone home before their parents arrived. Then use that feeling word with an example of feeling alone in the present.

CAUTIONS

There are two ways you should not approach this exercise:

- Do not use the same feeling word day after day. Doing this will lessen the effectiveness of the exercise to develop intimacy.

- Do not use one childhood memory for twenty different feeling words. Though several feeling words could describe one situation, it will be more effective to share as many different situations as possible with your spouse in the interest of developing emotional intimacy.

COMMON QUESTIONS

There are two common questions that couples ask.

"How should we choose our feeling word?" It doesn't matter how you choose feeling words from the list. I warn couples not to go down the "A" list because it may be difficult to start with words such as *abandoned* and *aching*.

Some couples just close their eyes and choose a word from the list. Some choose a word that starts with "A" and the next day pick a word that begins with "B" and so on. Others just pick a number, such as nine, and choose every ninth feeling word. Some just choose a word from a feeling they experienced that particular day. Again, the method each person uses to choose his or her feeling word is not relevant to developing and maintaining intimacy.

"How many feeling words should we do a day?" I recommend two feeling words a day per person.

Alternate with each other as you each share situations with two different feeling words. The exercise will not take a lot of time each day, and you will be able to fit it into even busy schedules. Be sure to include the following guidelines to insure optimal benefit from the exercise.

GUIDELINES

The following guidelines will help remove some obstacles that couples have experienced during this exercise. Following these guidelines will help you progress to your goal of emotional intimacy more quickly and safely.

1. No examples about each other. Do not involve your feelings for your spouse, either positive or negative, *in this exercise*. During any other time of day you may, but not during the feelings exercise. If the feeling word you choose is *frustrated*, you can be frustrated with traffic, children, dog or anything else—but not with your wife. If you choose the word *cuddly*, you can feel cuddly with the children or the dog, but not with your wife.

It is very important not to violate this guideline in order for this exercise to be a safe, nonthreatening place for both of you. If your spouse inadvertently starts giving an example that involves you, kindly remind her that it doesn't count and ask her to give you another example. If a spouse continues to violate this principle, it may signal that there is not a real desire to develop intimacy. Some people say they want intimacy, just as they want to be a millionaire, but they are not willing to do the work involved to achieve the stated goal.

2. Maintain eye contact. Looking into each other's eyes

is an important guideline to follow as emotional intimacy begins to happen with your spouse. There is a lot of truth in the saying "The eyes are the window of the soul." When you look into your spouse's eyes, you see her.

For many Christian couples who have grown apart, it is difficult to remember the last time they looked each other in the eye for more than a few seconds. They have become used to talking *at* each other instead of talking *to* each other. They look down at the floor, the ceiling or right past their spouse. Jokingly, I say to them, "That was great to share that feeling with your shoe. Now let's try it again and share it with your spouse." We all laugh, but the spouse must repeat the feeling statement again. As couples practice making eye contact, it becomes more natural for them to do. Many couples find that this is a key to significant progress for them in their overall communication.

My wife, Lisa, has the biggest green eyes I have ever seen. To look into them is to see her soul, and for me to see her soul is what drives me crazy for her. As you practice this guideline to the feelings exercises, I pray that you will experience this dimension of emotional intimacy that transcends words.

3. No feedback for seventy-two hours. As your spouse shares her feelings with you, there must not be comments or nonverbal reactions to what she is sharing. This guideline is critical to keep the exercise safe for both spouses. When your spouse shares a feeling and you pump her for more information, she will feel threatened and will be less likely to continue this very important exercise.

A violation of the "no feedback" guideline would be to suggest that she "shouldn't feel that way." Don't verbally interpret or comment on what she shared. Just say thank you and go ahead with *your* next feeling word.

The "seventy-two-hour" rule is important to this "no feedback" guideline as well. Whatever is shared during the exercise *cannot* be discussed for seventy-two hours. This time limit adds to the sense of emotional safety for the couple.

EMOTIONAL INTIMACY REQUIRES A SAFE ZONE.

If you are going to share your heart of hearts with your spouse, you have to know above all else that your feelings will be safe with her. The feelings exercise isn't just about identifying and learning to communicate feelings with your spouse. It is designed to create times of safety with your spouse during which you can experience intimacy with each other as emotionally safe people.

As time goes by in a marriage that is emotionally unsafe, a spouse will choose not to be emotionally intimate. The need for emotional intimacy doesn't go away because of that choice. The spouse will just seek another emotional outlet—golf with the guys for him or lunch with the girls for her. I feel sad for couples who find their primary emotional intimacy outside of their marriage. Sometimes this need for intimacy causes the vulnerable spouse to seek emotional and sexual affairs.

In a marriage, if the feelings your wife shares with you get shoved back into her face during an argument, she will conclude that you are not a safe person to share her feelings with. Guess what that does to your hope for sexual success? If she feels emotionally unsafe, sex is not going to be a priority for her.

Following the seventy-two-hour rule will increase the sense of emotional safety in your relationship tremendously. In that safe atmosphere you will want to share your feelings with your spouse and enjoy the emotional intimacy that God desires for you to have. This safe emotional environment can be yours in weeks.

I'm a guy who did it, and I now reap the wonderful harvest of emotional intimacy with my wife. Lisa and I have practiced this feelings exercise for over fourteen years. I have experienced such safety with my wife, Lisa, in this area. Her acceptance of my feelings and heart without feedback during the exercise has made me conclude that she is the safest person on the planet for my heart. My soul is saturated with my wife. This satisfying emotional intimacy protects me from temptation and really makes my life fun.

Emotional intimacy requires a safe zone.

It's normal for Lisa and me even throughout the day to stop each other and share what we are feeling at the moment or what we feel about a life event that day. I know I can call Lisa anytime and share positive or not-so-comfortable feelings with her, and she can do the same with me as well. For me that is what emotional intimacy is about. It's the feeling of not being alone in this world but rather connected with my wife spiritually and emotionally.

DAILY #3—PRAISE AND NURTURING

This exercise addresses the God-given need each of us has for nurturing and praise. As parents we intuitively know our children need to hear us say "I love you"; "I'm proud of you"; "You're smart"; "Great job"; and so on. I don't know where we get the notion that as adults we don't need nurturing. Yes, adults are expected to be mature, but that doesn't exclude our need of nurturing. The Bible records Jesus' admonition for us to come to God like a child:

> And he said: "I tell you the truth, unless you change and become like little children, you will never enter the kingdom of heaven. Therefore, whoever humbles himself like this child is the greatest in the kingdom of heaven."
>
> —Matthew 18:3–4

The wonderful reality that we are the sons and daughters—children—of God is a consistent theme throughout God's Word. And He knows the need of His children for affirmation and nurturing. He is infinite, and we are so terribly finite. I hope I never think I'm an adult who can act independently from God. Actually, the older I become the more childlike before God I am. I am a child of God, and I still need (not just want) praise and affirmation. When the Scriptures reveal the Father talking to Jesus, He is always affirming His love for His Son.

As a husband, you are the primary voice in your wife's life. A silent voice is the most cruel weapon you can use against your wife. The wife who hears neither bad nor good from her husband to whom she committed her life develops a hollowness in her emotions.

If our goal is to be like our Father in heaven (and that should be the goal of us all), then part of His nature flowing through us will be the nurturing and praising of others. Again, I realize from my own childhood that not everyone grew up receiving praise and nurturing from our families. So it is a skill that we must learn as adults.

Praise and nurturing one another is an essential ingredient for a vibrant, ongoing intimate relationship, which aids our sexual success. As you practice praise and nurturing, you will become skilled and comfortable with the ability to give emotional affirmation as well as receive it. For some husbands and wives it is giving praise that is difficult. For others, receiving praise is more difficult than giving it. Still others find that both giving praise and receiving praise are difficult.

Being able to give and receive praise is an acquired skill. And skills can be learned by everyone. Everyone can learn to praise and nurture a soul. As you practice this exercise daily, you and your spouse will experience the oil of intimacy dripping into your soul and healing areas of dryness that you didn't even know existed.

When I counsel couples I ask them to tell me the last

time they received a real heartfelt, eye-to-eye compliment, not just the obligatory "Thanks, honey." They pause for a moment, look at each other and then shrug their shoulders. This is sad because they don't know what they are missing; this is the icing on the cake for me. When Lisa tells me something positive about myself, which is almost every day, my soul leaps. I feel affirmed and strengthened to take on another day of life events. This is because I know in the depths of my heart that at the end of the worst day of my life, those big, green eyes of hers are going to look right into my heart and speak a loving affirmation to me.

Now I ask you, how hard do you think it is to be around someone who affirms you at least daily? Not hard at all, is my answer. We all love being around people who think that we're special or praiseworthy. It is even greater when that person is your spouse.

Imagine that you were going to take a very long journey, and you could choose between three spouses to travel with you. Spouse number one whom you could choose is critical of you the majority of the time. According to her, you don't know enough, you don't do things right, and you can't make her happy no matter what you do. I call this hell on earth.

The second spouse you could choose for your journey is silent most of the time. She doesn't praise or compliment you or really give you much of an opinion at all. Her gifts are all locked up inside in her fear, and she feels too inferior to be a helpmate. So you get to do it all—spiritually, emotionally, sexually and financially. This is what I call purgatory on earth. It isn't hell, because at least you are in control, but it sure is lonely.

The last spouse you could choose for your long journey knows how to compliment your personal qualities as a man. She can stop on even the busiest day to offer a kind word, and she has learned the discipline of seeing the good in you. I call this heaven on earth because your wife thinks and acts like God who created and saved you.

If these were your choices, which spouse would you choose? Spouse #1, spouse #2 or spouse #3? I am sure most of you would like to be stuck with spouse #3 for the journey of forty or fifty years together, if only you could start over again.

The great news is you do get to start all over again. The other side of the news is that you also need to become spouse #3—to your wife. Isn't it great that in a free society you can choose to be spouse #3 by bringing praise and nurturing to one of God's most special children, your wife? I can tell you that I have before God chosen to be spouse #3 to my wife, Lisa. Do you remember the principle of sowing and reaping we talked about earlier? Sowing praise into your wife will reap a harvest of nurturing and praise for you as well.

GUIDELINES

The guidelines for this exercise are similar to the guidelines for the feelings exercise. Both spouses think of two things that you love, appreciate or value about the other person. Then one spouse will begin by telling the other simply (praise) one of those things you value. The praise can apply to something he or she did during the day or can simply be something you appreciate in your spouse. When you both have two praises ready to share, you can begin this exercise.

Let's suppose the husband goes first. The guideline of maintaining eye contact with your spouse applies here as well. The husband looks into his wife's eyes and states, "I really appreciate that you are such a thrifty person. I like the way you saved us money on checking into the mortgage insurance today."

The wife continues to look into her husband's eyes until she accepts his praise, letting it into her heart. I purposely used the term *heart* and not *head*. This is not a cognitive exercise but a heart exercise. After the wife has let her husband's praise into her heart she says, "Thank you."

Saying "thank you" is an important part of the exercise. That is the moment when the recipient has received the praise in his or her heart. I used the word *received* because at first you may not agree with your spouse's praise, due to the lack of skill with which it is given. Or perhaps feelings of inferiority do not let you readily receive praise. So by saying "thank you" you acknowledge that you choose to receive this praise into your heart.

Then it is the wife's turn to give her husband his praise. As he maintains eye contact with his wife, he lets it into his heart and says, "Thank you." He then gives his wife a second praise, and she gives him a second praise, both with the follow-up words, "Thank you." If you want to get a feel for how this is done, refer to the example in the following illustration.

This is a sweet exercise that may seem simple, but for some couples, it is difficult work. Perseverance in this exercise, especially when combined with the other two dailies—prayer and the feelings exercise—can make a profound improvement in your intimacy.

Trent:	I really appreciate the extra effort you made today in completing the decorating project.
Natalie:	Thank you.
Natalie:	What I really love about you is that you are sincere about working on our marriage.
Trent:	Thank you.
Trent:	I love the way you laugh; it brings me such happiness to hear your laughter.
Natalie:	Thank you.
Natalie:	I appreciate you making time for me at lunch today.

Trent: Thank you.

REVIEWING THE THREE DAILIES

We have discussed at length the powerful three dailies that can form a safe structure to develop emotional intimacy with your wife. To review briefly, they are:

1. Pray daily with your spouse.

2. Do two feelings exercises, following these guidelines: no example about each other, maintain eye contact and no feedback.

3. Do two praises daily with eye contact; follow up with "Thank you."

Reading an example of a real conversation between a couple actually doing all three exercises is helpful for some couples to learn what to expect. Please refer to Appendix C for a sample conversation of all three dailies.

I want to add a personal note of testimony. I would never ask you to do something that my wife and I have not done or are not doing presently in our relationship. Two of the three dailies Lisa and I have done every day (with only a few exceptions) for over fourteen years. Since I developed the third daily involving nurturing praise, we have applied this healing exercise in our marriage as well.

Lisa and I maintain our relational priorities by practicing these three exercises daily. They are part of our bedtime routine. Neither of us expects to go to sleep without our relational ritual of the three dailies. I can tell you this is a major highlight of my day. I get to hear about my wife's day—really hear her heart. And she gets to hear about my day and look into my heart as well.

This relational structure has developed our skill for intimacy to a level that helps us weather the day-to-day challenges of children, writing and media demands as well as other commitments of life. There is not one person who knows me on any level who is not aware of my passion for Lisa. I love her, love her and really like her as well. This passion is the fruit of love that is nurtured through simple disciplines.

And that's it—the three dailies! I pray that you will allow this structure for emotional intimacy to work for you. As you develop the skills it offers, it will act as a "cast" to bring healing to your marriage. May God truly bless all the sowing that you have invested into your marriage, and may the harvest you reap be a blessing to the generations that follow you.

As you incorporate the three dailies in your marriage, your priorities for emotional intimacy will be restored, and consequently, passion will be restored as well. Keeping the emotional and spiritual intimacy warm makes sexual success much more possible.

ELEVEN

Sexual Agreement

A married couple will probably experience sex anywhere from two to five thousand times during the course of their marriage. As we have discussed, God made sex for marriage partners to enjoy and to celebrate each other. If couples learn to experience three-dimensional sex consistently, they can enjoy what I call God's best sex.

We have stated that the gift of God to man is a strong sex drive that doesn't quit until death. This drive motivates us to overrule our insecurities and self-doubts in order to start dating. It is a major motivation for men to marry, regardless of their spiritual maturity. A man's sex drive compels him to consistently work through the marital issues he faces during his entire lifetime. This God-given gift of sex is what glues a man to a woman tri-dimensionally: spiritually, emotionally and neurologically. A man's sexual drive is a great gift from God that brings with it many virtues.

For a woman, the gift of her sex drive motivates her differently. The woman's sex drive motivates her to desire the communion of an emotional and spiritual dimension with her man. Generally speaking, when she feels close to him she wants to express that closeness sexually. When she is being sexual, she is not looking for a sex act; she is looking for a love event. I believe a woman intuitively desires three-dimensional sex—spirit, soul and body—in the majority of her sexual experiences. Her gift of sexuality makes communion from her soul as important to her as the husband's physiological sex drive is to him.

God made sex for husband and wife to enjoy and celebrate each other. It is sad to me that with all this potential to please each other and experience the absolute joy of sex, couples cite their unhappiness in their sexual relationship as one of the top reasons they come in for marital counseling.

It amazes me continually that most of these couples I counsel admit that they have not discussed their sexual problem in a calm, rational way. Sometimes help is as close as one real conversation about their sexual expectations. Sexual agreement does not happen automatically for many couples. But when it is responsibly discussed and agreement is reached, sexual success is not far away.

You might not believe how often couples who come for counseling, regardless of how long they have been married, can't even agree on how often they are having sex. Their differences in perception are amusing when I ask them how often they are being sexually active together. Inevitably one spouse will say they are sexually active every ten to fourteen days. The other spouse will say twice a week. I have to chuckle when this happens and affirm to the couple that they are perfectly normal in their inability to agree on this issue.

Another interesting issue that arises while discussing with couples their sexual patterns is the frequency that each spouse desires to be sexual with his or her partner. Amy and Fred came to see me about some of these issues in their marriage. They were married for several years when they began to consider divorce. Fred was just finishing his degree to become a chiropractor. Amy had been supporting the family financially while Fred was in school and was feeling very neglected. They were having sex once every six to eight weeks. Amy and Fred were in their thirties. An average couple their age would typically be sexual about two to three times a week, which put this couple way off the scale of normalcy for their age group.

Amy and Fred loved each other and were active church members. Yet they said they argued about their sex life all the time. They wanted to stop this incessant fighting, and the only solution they could think of was divorce. They had two children and didn't want to divorce. Except for this sexual issue, they got along fine.

I asked Amy and Fred to write down separately on a piece of paper how often each of them would like to be sexual. When Amy flipped her piece of paper over it read that she wanted to be sexual two or three times a week. Fred flipped his paper over and, as you may have guessed, it said two or three times a week. We were all amused and relieved, realizing how easy it was going to be to save this marriage.

I asked Fred and Amy to explain to me why they were only having sex every six weeks when they both wanted to be sexual two or three times a week. Their answers were similar. They said that when they have sex, it's great. But then a few days go by, and neither one initiates sex. They start thinking their spouse doesn't want sex; if they did, they would ask to be sexual. A week goes by, and both spouses begin to feel unwanted and rejected by the other. Instead of sharing these feelings, they start to distance themselves from each other.

Eventually they both get irritable with each other, and as more time goes by, their angry outbursts increase over almost anything. Another week goes by, and they are so mad at each other that they feel guilty and eventually apologize. They make up and are sexual again. They feel great, but neither one initiates sex again for a few days, and the pattern repeats itself.

As we talked about their sexual pattern, Amy and Fred

realized some important things about their problem. First, they realized they had never calmly discussed together their mutual desire to be sexual in terms of frequency. And they learned that both were 100 percent responsible for the initiation of sex. Neither one had taken responsibility for their mutual sexuality; they had regarded their spouse as completely responsible to initiate sex. Third, they learned that it was possible to walk in agreement sexually and that doing so would probably mean they could be happy the rest of their lives together.

When assisting couples toward reaching sexual agreement and harmony, I ask this simple question of how often they would like to have sex. It is surprising how many times their answers are the same. They look at each other in amazement, and then say to me that they really didn't know they agreed so closely on the issue. My next question is usually, "Then why aren't you doing it that often?" Typically their answer is that they haven't had any real discussion or communication about the issue.

SEXUAL CHAOS VS. SEXUAL ORDER

How do painful situations like this happen? How can a couple remain married, in love and yet struggle so much in the area of sexuality? Here is what I believe happens to so many couples just like Amy and Fred.

For six months to a year after a couple gets married sex is usually not a problem issue. Both spouses are having plenty of sex and feel relatively good about the frequency of their sexual expression. As a couple takes on more responsibilities such as school, work, children, two cars and a mortgage, life becomes more stressful and complicated.

During the next few years, without the couple discussing it, a system of chaos and manipulation evolves. As the husband realizes that sex is beginning to slow down, he concludes, "If I ask for more, then I will get more. If I ask twice, and I am refused once, I only have sex once. If I ask four times, I can at least get sex twice, and if I am lucky maybe three times." As this brave young male smartens up sexually, the dance of manipulation begins.

During a marriage, either consciously or unconsciously, every couple develops a sexual system.

When his wife begins to feel her husband's pressure to be sexual, she starts drawing some conclusions about sex and her husband. When he starts with kissing and hugging in the kitchen, she thinks if she lets him do that he will think she wants to be sexual. She decides not to let him kiss and hug her so he won't ask for sex. She begins to manipulate how much affection she will participate in, hoping in this way to manage the sexuality in her young marriage.

Manipulation can get even more complicated as the couple tries to deal with their sexual life together without talking about it. When I was a teenager I remember seeing a plaque in a store that had two dials, one for him and one for her. The sayings around the dial read "not tonight," "no way," "I'm tired," "if you hold me first," "maybe," "ask and take your chance," "OK, if I have to," and "tonight's your night." As a young man I remember thinking how confusing this sex thing must be. As a more experienced adult, I don't think it has to be that difficult.

During a marriage, either consciously or unconsciously, every couple develops a sexual system. This system gives them a way to figure out how to ask without asking and how to reject without communicating. Unfortunately, these systems are many times unclear even to the couples participating in the sexual system they created.

Even the best of Christian marriages can falter and spouses injure each other through years of marriage where there is a non-discussed and non-agreed upon sexual system, one that is co-created but for which no one takes responsibility.

Taking responsibility is an important factor for successful sexuality in marriage. As we have discussed, the fact that someone is physically an adult does not mean he or she is a sexual adult. Sexual adults take responsibility for their sexuality. In part, that means to create a workable agreement for their sexual expression that is understood by and acceptable to both spouses.

SEXUAL ACCEPTANCE

If a couple can accept the different motivational force each of their sexuality reflects, and not try to manipulate their spouse's gift of sexuality, they will move more quickly toward creating the best sex of their life. Sexual acceptance is a key to reaching the shared goal of sexual success.

I vividly remember a conversation I had years ago with a client about his sexuality issues with his wife. He was a thirty-year-old professional with three children and a stay-at-home wife. He and his wife were having sex very infrequently. I shared with him the emotional needs of women to feel close to their man before wanting to be sexual.

He said to me, "You're right!" He had read a book recently about women's emotional needs. It instructed men to listen to their wives without trying to solve the problem. The book also suggested that they ask their wives about her feelings and share their own feelings with her without being prompted. He said to me, "I did everything the book told me to do for three months. And we were having the most and best sex of our marriage!" So I asked him, "What happened?" His thoughtful response has stayed with me all these years. "I stopped doing my part," he said.

For three months this husband had accepted the fact that men are different from women. He gave his wife the emotional intimacy she needed to celebrate sexual intimacy with her husband. And the rewards were great, according to his testimony. Yet he had somehow forgotten to treat his wife as a woman in her sexuality, and he was suffering the consequences in his marriage.

Women have emotional needs that men don't necessarily have at the same level. A major part of the wife's sexuality is wrapped up in getting her spiritual and emotional needs met on a daily basis. When wise husbands make this happen, they experience the transformation of their wives' spiritual, emotional and sexual demeanor. Husbands who consistently give their wives the oil of intimacy will see that sexuality is more comfortable for her to participate in and initiate. Learning to live in an atmosphere of sexual acceptance with his wife will pay wonderful dividends for life.

When a couple decides to act responsibly as sexual adults, a sense of peace floods their mutual sexuality.

In contrast, men are pretty simple in their thought process about sex. A man's sexuality is centered in a desire to be touched and to touch. All men are sexual; most men are very sexual. That will not change! Men think about sex almost as much as they think about food; they are creatures of appetite. These appetites create positive motivation for men to work diligently to provide for their needs and the needs of their family. They understand if you don't work, you don't eat. And if you don't establish a family, you don't get your sexual needs met, at least not in a healthy way.

If a man marries and finds that the sexual system he and his wife share, knowingly or unknowingly, is based on manipulation, then he has to develop finely tuned skills to manipulate his wife into sex. This unhealthy system creates a state of constant "sexual anxiety" for the husband. His God-given gift of sexuality that motivates him to marry is not being satisfied by his wife. He doesn't know when he will have sex, which creates a real anxiety that makes him think about it more than if he were secure in a mutual understanding or agreement about being sexual with his wife.

When a man knows when sex can occur and who is initiating it, he thinks about sex a lot less and suffers almost no sexual anxiety. A wife who has become an adult sexually and takes responsibility to accept her husband sexually will create a secure atmosphere for the intimacy she desires. Sexual acceptance is an important key to creating a sexual agreement that will bring a couple to successful sexuality.

SEXUAL AGREEMENT

A sexual agreement is reached by a couple who intelligently and calmly discusses their sexual preferences regarding issues of frequency, who initiates being sexual and other guidelines for their mutual sexuality. They then distribute the responsibility between them for initiating sex fairly based on their agreement. Both husband and wife agree to their discussed choices of sexual expression with each other. Then they write their guidelines for structuring their sexuality in a way that both spouses can expect to be reasonably satisfied.

When a couple decides to act responsibly as sexual adults and enter into a sexual agreement in which they keep their word to each other, a sense of peace floods their mutual sexuality. Remember that both male and female sexuality are a gift from God. They are to be accepted and celebrated, not simply tolerated, by both husband and wife.

A man who feels sexually tolerated by his wife will become resentful and generate many other negative feelings toward her. On the other hand, a woman who feels used by her husband, without consideration of her emotional intimacy needs, will make their sexual encounters more infrequent and less satisfying. Spouses who offer sexual acceptance and celebration to each other will have an ongoing positive feeling and expression of love in their marriage.

Let me offer a word of caution to husbands. Don't discuss the concept of a sexual agreement with your wife until you have been consistent in practicing the three daily exercises for sixty to ninety days. You may get only one chance to discuss it. If your wife is spiritually and emotionally distant because of your lack of intimacy skills or your neglect, it may backfire. She will quickly see through your plot to get more sex without meeting her needs first. She may feel you are manipulative, lazy and weak.

So first things first, men. Do the intimacy exercises to establish caring communication, and then talk about a sexual agreement. Success in life is about negotiation. This is especially true in marriage. It is unreasonable and selfish for a man to pester his wife to have sex daily; it is also unreasonable and selfish for a wife to want sex only one time a month. Creating a sexual agreement can bring health and success into your relationship when you pay the price to meet the criteria we have discussed.

CREATING A SEXUAL AGREEMENT

The biblical principle for walking in sexual agreement can be found in the prophet's rhetorical question, "Can two walk together, except they be agreed?" (Amos 3:3, KJV). The obvious response is no. If you don't deliberately agree with your spouse on a sexual system, you cannot hope to reach your goal of sexual success. There are exceptions, of course, for some couples who are fortunate that their unconsciously evolved sexual system satisfies both spouses. But for most couples, creating a sexual agreement is a necessary.

Management structures are used in almost every other area of your life. In finances, you organize, manage and oversee a system of money management. You also manage the raising of your children. Your spiritual and emotional lives require many agreements and systems. Much of life is about effective management for optimal results. This is also true in creating a sexual agreement with your spouse that will bring peace to your marriage.

Don't discuss the concept of a sexual agreement with your wife until you have been consistent in practicing the three daily exercises for sixty to ninety days.

As you walk through the process of creating a sexual agreement together, it is important to do the following:

- Be open-minded to each other's needs sexually.

- Be honest about your sexuality.

- If you can't do this together, get professional help.

THE FREQUENCY AND INITIATION ISSUES

One of the first issues you will need to address in creating a sexual agreement is the frequency of being sexual. Both of you will need to write on a piece of paper your own personal preferences. For a reference point, you may want to know that the average frequency for a couple up to the age of about fifty is between one to three times a week. After that age, sexual frequency usually lessens to about once a week.

The issue of who will initiate being sexual is sometimes not considered because the husband has always been the primary or only sexual initiator. There are tremendous benefits to deciding that both spouses will be responsible to initiate your sexual experiences.

Many men have experienced years of being totally responsible for the sexuality in their marriage. They have felt tolerated by their wife, as if they had a disease for which the medicine was having sex. When a couple decides that both will initiate their sexual experiences, the husband has the opportunity to receive sexual initiation from his wife, which makes him feel wanted and valued as a sexual partner like never before.

Too often wives feel that they have no sexual choices except to submit sexually to their husband. They become defensive, avoiding their husband's affections because they do not want to be sexual later. When a wife feels that her choice to be sexual has been stifled, sexual agreement frees her to feel that *This is my sexuality, and this is how I want to express it.* A woman feels her own sexuality is returned to her when she has a choice to initiate their intimate time together.

You will need to negotiate these issues of frequency and initiation together. This is *your* marital sexual system, so you can be as creative as you wish. If one spouse prefers to be sexual twice a week and the other spouse wants to be sexual three times a week, you can each initiate your frequency preference during your week.

I usually ask couples to keep their agreement for a minimum of ninety days to see if the system is working for them. If the system needs changing at that point, it is important to discuss the change in a public place (not your bedroom or in your house). In that way it will not be perceived as a manipulation of one trying to pressure their spouse into more or less sexuality than they agreed to. The following basic sexual systems may help you to choose a system that will work best for you.

System one

To initiate this system of sexual responsibility, simply choose the days that you want to be sexual after coming to agreement concerning the frequency you will be sexual. If you want to be sexual twice a week, choose any two days of the week that work best for your schedule and agree on them. For example, if Jason and Dana choose to be sexual two days a week on Tuesday and Saturday, Jason could be responsible to initiate on Tuesdays and Dana could be responsible for initiating on Saturdays.

Another way to divide their sexual responsibility would be for Jason to choose the first and third week of the month to initiate and Dana the second and fourth week. Some couples love this system because they don't have to concern themselves about whose turn it is. And it lends itself to a busy schedule because on their busier days they both can decide to be stress free concerning sexuality. Other couples find this system too rigid and not spontaneous enough for their style.

System two

In this system of choosing when to be sexual, you would divide the week between you. If you agreed to be sexual twice a week, John would decide on Sunday, Monday or Tuesday to initiate sex one time during this three-day period. Wednesday would be off for both of you in a twice-a-week system, although some couples make Wednesday a day that either can ask. Dana would choose to initiate one time on Thursday, Friday or Saturday of that week. Some couples love the flexibility this system allows for a person to choose when they want to be sexual.

System three

In this rotating system, a spouse can initiate sex during any one of their days. If you decided on being sexual twice a week, each person has three days to initiate sex with their spouse (day one, two or three). The day after they initiate, the other spouse's days to initiate begin, and they also have three days (day one, two or three) to initiate. In this system, if Jason decides to wait until day two, then on what would have been his day three, it is Dana's turn. She can initiate on day one of her turn or wait until day three. If Dana decides to initiate on day one, the couple has been sexual two consecutive days. Then it is Jason's turn again. He may decide to wait until day three to initiate his turn.

This system provides both the utmost of flexibility for those couples wanting spontaneity, as well as accommodating higher frequency of sexuality in their relationship. In this system, you can have sex as little as twice a week (both spouses waiting for the third day to initiate) or daily or anywhere in between. Again, for some couples this system is ideal, but for others it's too fluid.

The sexual system you choose, or whether you design your own unique system, is not as important as the fact that you have chosen to walk in agreement sexually. Sexual agreement is such a blessing to couples because it gives them a sincere taste of sexual harmony and peace. I know from my experience as a Christian marriage and family counselor that where the spirit of the Lord is, there is freedom (2 Cor. 3:17). Too often Christian marriages do not reflect this freedom from conflict; there is no peace in the bedroom. Sadly, many times this is true not because of a lack of love or even a lack of sexual desire, but simply because of a lack of agreement.

BENEFITS OF AGREEMENT

The benefits of walking in sexual agreement are tremendous. I can tell you from my own life experience that walking in this concept has brought much clarity and peace into our marriage since we have implemented it. I have also seen the tremendous amount of peace that sexual agreement has brought to many of the Christian couples whom

I have counseled over the last ten years, since we have been teaching sexual agreement systems.

FOR YOU

Sexual anxiety is reduced dramatically for husbands who have a sexual agreement in their marriage. The husband rests in the knowledge that he is going to be sexual on a regular basis. Your fear of being rejected is gone. And you no longer feel the need to be manipulative to get sex.

You can also know approximately how often and when you will be sexual with your wife, which is very important to us as men. Your God-given need to be sexually fed has been heard, understood and agreed upon by the person you love most—your wife.

The fact that your wife is now going to initiate some of your sexual encounters is also a wonderful benefit for the husband. As we have explained, this is an important part of your feeling wanted, needed and valued by your wife.

Faithfulness to fulfill a sexual system fairly gives you a much greater respect and appreciation for your wife. She becomes more precious and desirable in your heart. You feel comforted in the knowledge that *she's in this with me.* You don't feel alone sexually.

I can't tell you how many men pull me aside and say things like, "I've never been this in love with my wife," simply because of having a sexual system in place. And they are not referring just to sexual frequency. They mean the sense of unity and love they feel toward their wife because they are walking together in sexual agreement—finally.

FOR HER

The benefit of being in sexual agreement greatly affects the wife as well. I can relate the relief many wives have expressed in counseling sessions just to finally have a place of agreement that was predictable in their sexuality issues. Many of them felt hopeless and frustrated trying to manage both their own and their husband's sexuality. These wives who now have sexual agreement systems in place within their marriage have shared several specific benefits with me.

First, they are happy that their own sexuality has been returned to them. God made every woman to be sexual as well as men. But many wives feel they always have to respond to his sexuality so much that they don't have the opportunity to express their own sexuality. Combined with the ambivalence of not knowing how far things are going to go sexually in response to their husband's advances, wives become frustrated in their sexual expression.

The new sense that *This is my sexuality, and this is how I want to express it* is a great benefit for a woman who has entered into a sexual agreement with her husband. She can choose her time (within limits) to decide when she will be sexual.

A wife who has a sexual agreement in place can also relax with her husband's spontaneous hugs and kisses. She is ready to respond if it is time for him to initiate their being sexual as they have agreed. When it's her turn to initiate, she knows it will only become sexual by her choice. This allows her to receive his affection into her heart instead of feeling as if she has to defend herself from further advances. This freedom not to be sexual is as valuable a benefit as the freedom to be sexual in her way.

Her sexual desires have also been heard and accepted by the love of her life—her husband. She is a respected equal in their sexual system, which helps her to respect herself. She is living as a sexual adult who doesn't need to be manipulated or coerced to be sexual.

FOR BOTH

I have watched numerous couples' intimacy increase significantly after they have been consistent with a sexual system. This sexual issue has been a drain on both the husband and the wife in their marriage. They no longer have to manipulate, argue, fuss or pout about sex anymore. This peace can give couples a lot more energy to just love each other and enjoy their lives together.

Another benefit to couples having a sexual system in place is heightened sexual esteem. Both husband and wife have a new sense of sexual confidence and awareness, knowing that they are not only being satisfied sexually but are also sexually satisfying their mate. It is intricate to your self-esteem to feel good about your sexuality and its expression.

As part of initiating your sexual agreement, you need to set consequences for failure to comply.

A last benefit I have seen in couples who walk in sexual agreement is a removal of sexual controlling authority from one person in the relationship. In a sense the agreement becomes the authority, not the husband or wife who in the past controlled or dominated their sexuality. Neither spouse can be blamed for what they have agreed to together. Couples are more likely to submit to the authority of an agreement that they participated in creating.

Although a sexual agreement may be challenging to keep for those who have been living irresponsibly as sexual children or sexual adolescents, the journey's end will be worth any difficulty. After a while, I am sure you will find the experience positive as you and your spouse learn to walk in sexual agreement.

PRACTICAL GUIDELINES FOR SUCCESS

NO EXCUSES

To your spouse's sexual advances, you must *always* say *yes* unless you have a doctor's excuse! You know when your spouse is too sick to be sexual. As a Christian, you must be considerate of that. But beyond that, the "I'm tired" or "I have a headache" lies don't work in a sexual agreement.

CONSEQUENCES

Change can be difficult, especially for those who have struggled with sexual addiction, sexual anorexia or just simple sexual immaturity issues. Even after you set up a sexual agreement, if your spouse doesn't keep his or her word, what do you do?

As part of initiating your sexual agreement, you need to set consequences for failure to comply. To qualify as consequence, the punishment must be distasteful to the spouse who transgressed. Each spouse should be allowed to choose their own consequence. Here are some examples of consequences that have been effective for other couples:

- Hand wash and detail the spouse's automobile.

- Volunteer two to four hours at a nursing home.

- Send $100 donation to the local political party to which you are most opposed.

- Volunteer at the local political party to which you are most opposed.

- Spend time with a relative you don't like.

- Send money to a relative or organization you don't like.

- Run two miles.

- Give your spouse a sixty- to ninety-minute massage.

- Watch the children for four hours while your spouse goes somewhere.

- Don't watch sports for two weeks.

- Don't go hunting or fishing.

- Make a counseling appointment.

Both spouses decide what their consequence would be for not fully participating in their sexual agreement. For example, if John withholds sex from Mary when it is his turn to initiate, he would complete his consequence. Likewise, if Mary refuses John when he initiates properly, she completes her agreed-upon consequence. If a person refuses to do their consequence or if one person is regularly not keeping their sexual word, then I would strongly suggest getting professional counsel.

WAIT YOUR TURN!

When it is *not* your turn, *you cannot ask!* This is a simple guideline, but when someone consistently doesn't respect the sexual space of the other person, it erodes the effectiveness of the sexual system.

HER SPECIAL DAYS

It is important for a couple to communicate clearly in two areas regarding the wife's menstrual cycle. First, agree on what is expected and acceptable sexually during these days, and second, decide how the arrival of this cycle should be communicated to the husband. These are options couples have chosen:

- To continue sexually as normal

- To suspend sexual activity for a defined period (i.e., so many days or so many turns at initiating)

- Be sexual but have no intercourse

Any of these options should be agreed upon to avoid misunderstanding. Also, it is important to communicate this potential disappointment in a timely and sensitive way. It is not fair to the husband, who has been thinking about being sexual with his wife all day, to come home for dinner, help with the children's homework, get them bathed and in bed, and then jump into bed with his beloved only to hear her she say she can't; she started her period that morning.

If he responds with anything less than "I hope you are feeling OK," he will be cast as insensitive and selfish. While she can't do anything about getting her period and should not be made to feel "less than" during this time, clear communication can help both partners to cope. Here are some ways couples have agreed to handle the news:

1. To let her husband know as soon as she finds out.

2. Send an e-mail with a catch phrase.

3. Tell him when he comes home, before dinner.

4. Tell him after dinner but before homework.

Clear communication can save ill feelings that result, not from the fact of the menstrual cycle, but from the unexpected change in the sexual agreement. Agree to a preventative measure to avoid any disappointments.

Mutual satisfaction

As we stated earlier, people vary in their sexual personalities, preferences, histories and the amount of sexual sin they have participated in. You must agree on sexual behaviors that are mutually satisfying and acceptable to both spouses.

Since this is going to be the only garden of sexuality you will both be eating from, it is helpful for you both to define what is acceptable. Some fruit may be acceptable all the time, others you can have sometimes (decide who can initiate that particular fruit), and some fruit is definitely forbidden.

On a separate sheet of paper, you can write out the various fruits of your sexual expression that each of you desires.

Below you can indicate what is acceptable for each spouse or both.

Example	He			She		
	Yes	No	Only if I initiate	Yes	No	Only if I Initiate
Position 1	❑	❑	❑	❑	❑	❑
	Yes	No	Only if I initiate	Yes	No	Only if I initiate
Position 2	❑	❑	❑	❑	❑	❑
	Yes	No	Only if I initiate	Yes	No	Only if I initiate
Act A	❑	❑	❑	❑	❑	❑
	Yes	No	Only if I initiate	Yes	No	Only if I initiate
Act B	❑	❑	❑	❑	❑	❑
	Yes	No	Only if I initiate	Yes	No	Only if I initiate
Place 1	❑	❑	❑	❑	❑	❑
	Yes	No	Only if I initiate	Yes	No	Only if I initiate
Place 2	❑	❑	❑	❑	❑	❑

After you write out the possibilities, both of you circle the appropriate response. Everything you both circle *yes* is a fruit that you agree on and can participate in with a clear conscious before God and each other.

The things you both circle *no* are things that would defile your particular garden and should never be asked for by either spouse. When one spouse answers *yes* and the other answers *no*, these are areas of sexual disagreement. You would not participate in or ask for these either during sex because you do not agree.

If you feel some areas of disagreement need further discussion, you can seek out a counselor or a pastor in your area. The purpose of the counseling would be to hear the rationales and histories and to see if this is a negotiable behavior, not to manipulate your spouse to do what you want sexually.

The column that states *only if I initiate* can be used by a spouse who does not want to participate in this behavior, but to please their spouse they are willing to do so occasionally. Though it is not sinful, your spouse is simply not comfortable with it.

Sometimes an example helps to clarify a general concept that you can apply specifically to another situation in your life. For the response of *only if I initiate* that applies to your sexual behavior with your spouse, it may be helpful to some to read Charles and Cindy's story.

~

Charles and Cindy are a middle-aged Christian couple who have raised two teenagers. Overall, Charles and Cindy have a good Christian marriage and had successfully worked on most areas of their relationship. There is one sexual issue that has continually caused some turmoil in their relationship. They came to counseling to resolve this one issue that involved a particular sexual behavior Charles liked but Cindy was not comfortable with.

Charles liked for Cindy to wear fancy, sexy lingerie. Charles enjoyed his wife's body and liked the way she looked in the lingerie. Cindy, however, was more conservative in her sexual personality and said she did not feel like a Christian wife, but a prostitute when she dressed in the lingerie that Charles liked.

Cindy's conflict went deeper in her psyche. She felt that Charles didn't think she was sexy enough to please him without dressing in a way that was out of character for her. Cindy felt she was being coerced into this behavior in order to please her husband.

The problem issue wasn't the act itself; it was the feelings and perceptions that the act provoked. As we talked, she realized that she could do this once in a while, but only if she picked out the clothes and only "when she initiated" that she wanted to express her sexuality that way. When Cindy felt free to choose and express herself and understood that she was loved whether she wore these clothes or not, then she felt more comfortable wearing them occasionally.

~

The column that states "only if I initiate" is designed for the type of a situation in which Cindy and Charles found themselves. Agreement on what fruits are acceptable to both partners can add a greater sense of safety and trust in the area of sexuality. When you both agree, there can be freedom and fun in the areas of sexuality.

TIME LIMIT FOR CHANGES

You must agree with your spouse that that the system stays in place for at least sixty to ninety days before changing any aspect of it. Also, one spouse may not make changes in the sexual agreement; both spouses must agree for a change to be made. If you run into difficulties in any area, you may need a professional to navigate you through these changes. Some couples agree only to make changes in their sexual agreement if their pastor or counselor agree. Their counsel will minimize temptations to manipulation by one spouse or the other.

CHECKLIST FOR YOUR AGREEMENT

You have completed the instructions for creating a sexual system in your marriage. The following is a checklist you can use to determine when you have included the various ingredients to a successful sexual agreement.

❑ We have both written down our sexual agreement in a clear format that outlines how often sex is to occur.

❑ We have both written down who is responsible to initiate sexuality in a timely way.

❑ We have stated that we will say yes unless we have a doctor's excuse.

❑ We have included self-imposed consequences for both spouses if either does not keep their sexual agreements.

❑ We have included the "not asking when it's not your turn" policy.

❑ We have agreed to a plan about menstrual cycles and how we will communicate its arrival.

❑ We have a written agreement as to what is acceptable / not acceptable / only if I initiate behavior.

❑ We have a clause that tells us when our agreement can be changed.

If you completed all eight steps, you only have to decide when you want to start your sexual agreement. You can write the date in your agreement.

I understand from living in Colorado that to hike the mountains requires commitment and work. But it is also true that the higher you climb, the cleaner the air is that you breathe, the cooler the temperatures are and the more spectacular the view. I pray God's richest blessing on your marriage as you begin your climb by establishing your sexual agreement and begin to partake of all the fruits you have agreed upon. Your garden of intimacy is a great place for a couple to be, naked and unashamed in the presence of the Lord. It is what God intended for His creation:

> The man and his wife were both naked, and they felt no shame.
>
> —GENESIS 2:25

This journey to successful sexuality may seem to be more work than you bargained for. As a man, you not afraid of work, especially if everyone wins as a result of your focused efforts. You can definitely master the skills of intimacy and grow in areas where you have been deficient. And you can hold your head high because you are acting responsibly with the woman God gave you. As a man, during this process, you will not only be feeling sexually successful but also masculine. Though your climb to successful sexuality may be work, please let me encourage you as a fellow traveler, the view will be worth your every effort. May God bless your diligence!

TWELVE

Leaving a Legacy

One of the eternal blessings of becoming a Christian man who is sexually successful is leaving a positive and healthy legacy for your sons. Your sons look to you as a model in every area of their lives. How often do you take a moment to think what kind of sexual role model you are being for your son? It is your responsibility to talk with your sons about their sexuality. What do you say? When? Let's walk this leg of the journey together. I want every man to feel confident that he is impacting his family for the next generation with the sexual health he has achieved. This part of the trip may get challenging for some, but if you persevere, you could be instrumental in sparing your sons some of your pain and in changing the lives of your sons, your grandsons and future generations.

ROLE-MODELING

The way we role-model male sexuality is impacting our sons' interpretation of what comprises acceptable and unacceptable behavior. I have spent countless hours counseling men whose father's sexual role-modeling was either absent or worse still, destructive. The absent role model is the father who never discusses sexuality with his son. He acts as if he is not having sex at all. He doesn't know what to say about it, so he says nothing and hopes for the best.

The destructive role model is the father who treats his wife with disrespect in front of his son, talks to him about his affairs with other women and perhaps leaves his pornography lying around the house. Many young men get hooked on pornography from looking at their dad's stash of trash. Fathers may think they hide it, but young men can sniff that stuff out.

This type of role model is destructive to a young man's heart. He doesn't know whom to protect: Dad's secrets or the mother he loves. The destructive role model takes long, lingering looks at other women, letting his son believe that lust is normal sexual behavior; it's OK. This role model also makes comments about women's body parts and teaches his son that women are objects.

The way we role-model male sexuality is impacting our sons.

The entertainment he watches regularly contains sexual innuendoes that make him laugh and respond positively. This behavior sends a clear message that voyeurism through television and movies is acceptable, and listening to or watching this type of sexuality is normal. All of this negative role-modeling influences and molds a son's sexuality. In spite of all the sex talk this father indulges in, he has little to say during a sex talk with his son. His son is left on his own to figure out his sexuality.

The positive role model is one who is deliberate about communicating healthy sexuality to his son. He gets informed and looks for opportunities to talk about girls with his son in a positive way. He is behaviorally pure himself from pornography and adultery, and he teaches his son to respect his mother and sisters.

This Christian role model has been honest with other adult men about any lust issues in his life. He responsibly blocks the Internet, and he monitors television and media intake for himself and his family. He is emotionally connected to his son enough so that they can talk about sex. This father is a good, general role model for male sexuality.

Regardless of the kind of role model your father was for you, it is possible for you to become sexually successful and become a good role model for your sons. They will *catch* more of your sexuality from your life than they will learn from any book they read or video they watch. The areas of your life that are important communicators are:

- Your personal purity. If you struggle sexually, your shame can cripple you from effective, positive sexual role modeling.

- Your behavior and attitudes toward women in general. You can only teach respect for women if you have respect for women.

- Your media intake. If you are silent about sexual innuendoes, sexual immorality, adultery and inappropriate dress while with your son, in his eyes you are condoning this behavior.

- Your intentional sexual conversations with your sons.

If you are doing well as a role model, these areas will be communicating the message you desire your son to hear. If you're not, then begin now. Your personal sexuality is a large player in raising sexually healthy sons.

WHAT DO I SAY AND WHEN?

I want to alleviate some pressure here for you as a dad. Many men think in terms of having *the talk* with their sons. Such thinking is very limited and puts a lot of pressure on you to get it all right because you only have one shot at it. I think this paradigm is archaic. As a modern man, talking to your son is much different than it was a generation or two ago when kids married right out of high school.

Let's face it: Our sons may be single until their middle to late twenties. Our grandfathers hit puberty at eighteen and were married shortly thereafter. Our sons hit puberty at fourteen or earlier because of health advantages. They are part of the generation that will be sexually mature and single longer than any generation in the history of mankind. This is a major challenge to change our thinking in this area in order to raise them to be sexually healthy.

The positive role model is one who is deliberate about communicating healthy sexuality to his son.

Also, our sons have inherited a much more sexually stimulating culture than we and our fathers have known. Because of the blatant sexual idolatry in North America, our sons will see and hear more about sex in many more varieties of media than we did. That's without considering the Internet, a demon like no other that can trash a young boy's sexuality in seconds.

Before I go any farther, I want to state clearly that you are not 100 percent responsible for your son's sexual choices, or your daughter's for that matter. We all have a will, and humans are capable of making bad choices despite having the best information. Adam and Eve had God as a father, and they still erred. You are, however, 100 percent responsible for your role-modeling and for disciplining your son regarding sex.

Having said this, I want to discuss some of the issues involved in your role-modeling. The first issue today's fathers need to address is a paradigm shift from *the talk*, which we have mentioned, to the paradigm of *shepherding your son's sexuality*. As a Christian role model, you will be guiding him along the path of sexuality from twelve years old until marriage and beyond. Accepting this shepherding paradigm means you will be having hundreds of sexual conversations between his youth and marriage.

What to say exactly during these conversations could fill another book. However, I have prepared videos that cover many of these topics in more depth, including *Shepherding Your Sons Sexually* and *Good Enough to Wait*, a teen video you can view together with your sons and daughters.

In these few pages, I will list for you areas you should address with your sons to shepherd them into healthy sexuality. You will have to decide "when" based on their age, maturity and current exposure to sexual information. I believe most of this information should be covered by age fourteen. Here are some topics for conversation:

- The mechanics of sex—The concepts of the penis inside the vagina, ejaculation, sperm and pregnancy. Most sex education books cover all these issues.

- Sex and the brain—How the brain is conditioned and connects to what the eyes look at. (The video *Good Enough to Wait* covers this.)

- Internal and external sexuality—Go over Exodus 20 with your son and explain the tenth commandment. Do a word study on *lust* in the Bible. Explain the rubber-band technique.

- Sex only in the context of marriage—Refer to the Bible for this one.

- Bad women—Explain the dangers of women who want to steal his purity. Refer to the story of Samson, Proverbs 5, Revelation 2 and many others. Some teenage girls who are like the women described in these passages of Scripture can scar your son.

- Sexually transmitted diseases and their life-long consequences.

- Guidelines for courting or dating—Paul's admonition to treat all women as sisters and what that means.

- Dangers of pornography and the Internet—Block open access to the Internet in your home, and know the service providers of your son's friends if he frequents their homes.

- Condoms—The lie of safe sex.

- Masturbation.

Additionally, here are some resources for current and reliable information regarding sex:

- A local Christian high school health teacher

- The local health clinic

- Your wife's OB/GYN doctor

- Local Bible/Christian bookstores

- Focus on the Family, (719) 531-3400

- The SHARE Program, (425) 644-3312

If your church doesn't have any resources to teach Christian sexuality, you may want to share this list with them. When you find a good resource, purchase a second copy for the church to loan out to others. You can attend our father/son retreats also, where sexual topics are sometimes covered more thoroughly in a relaxed atmosphere.

MASTURBATION

Well, here we are again talking about the "M" word. That is because of the importance it is that you address this issue with your son. Even if you believe it is not necessary because your son is pure, or if you are reluctant because you have issues with sexuality yourself, remember, you are still 100 percent responsible to talk to your son. Your personality or preferences don't negate the fact that it's your job.

You might want to review the chapter on masturbation again before your talk. Make it a point to discuss the three types of masturbators. Remember, your young son doesn't have *your* history sexually; he has his own. Also clearly discuss the fact that lust is sin.

Let me be clear about this issue: I am not recommending masturbation for anyone. If you are reading this book, stop and say aloud, "Doug Weiss is not recommending masturbation." I don't want anyone calling me, e-mailing me or asking me if I condone masturbation. I know that as Christian men we all would like to believe our sons will never masturbate. But since the percentage of those in North America who don't is so incredibly small, we have to look at our options.

Your first option is to tell him nothing about masturbation. This leaves it up to your son to be informed about masturbation by his peers and the media sources of our American culture. Your neglect to say anything can also leave him feeling isolated and thinking he is the only one struggling with this issue. The second option is to give your son some sexual guidelines, define what is sin in a way he understands, and then hope and pray he will make wise choices.

For those who decide for the first option, nothing needs to be written. I would encourage you, however, to be sure of your reasons for this choice, and I hope you will read further. For those who choose the second option, I would suggest that you include a discussion about the following four guidelines for masturbation. (Again, repeat aloud, "Doug Weiss is not encouraging masturbation.") The fourth guideline listed here is the most important.

GUIDELINE 1: FREQUENCY

First, suggest limits to your son for the frequency of masturbation. Discuss how many times a week or month is acceptable. You're the dad, and you can come up with a number. When I am coaching dads, I suggest no more than once or twice a week. This is not to suggest that they do it that often, but to keep it to no more than this.

Why? When I talk to a teenager, I often have to break the news to him that the culture and the media are lying to him when they project that women want sex every day. For most women, one to two times a week is plenty. I explain that if he trains his body (through masturbation) to have sex four to seven times a week, and he does this for years, he will be frustrated in marriage when his wife doesn't meet his developed appetite for daily sex. Most likely the teen's future wife didn't masturbate. She will be clueless about his frustration. I encourage him not to set himself up for this inevitable conflict.

GUIDELINE 2: NO PORN OR FANTASY

At this point review the brain pathway information. (The *Good Enough to Wait* video is helpful here.) This will help your son understand that what he views while masturbating will set up a strong neuropathic desire for that specific object or person. Using pornography or fantasies can also establish beliefs that can become a detriment to how his wife thinks about sex.

Why? If you masturbate to pictures of models (pictures

that are airbrushed to make them look perfect and models who often have had numerous plastic surgeries) who are 6-foot-tall redheads, that is what you will chase. When God gives you a perfectly wonderful, godly woman who is 5 feet 2 inches tall with an average build, you will be unhappy with His gift to you. Don't fantasize about women because the fantasies will be different sexually from the woman you marry. This will aggravate you, and your wife will feel your unacceptance of her. She will be hurt and feel that her sex is not good enough for you.

GUIDELINE 3: STAY CONNECTED

If a young man stays with his body during masturbation and doesn't disconnect to a fantasy world, he can avoid lust.

Why? If you practice connected sexuality now, you will be able to enjoy connected sex with your future wife. Women want you present—mentally and emotionally, not just physically—when having sex. Disconnected sex is not only distasteful to women; it is undesirable. If you're planning to have sex for a lifetime, plan to have connected sex. If you practice disconnected masturbation, connected sex with a future wife will prove incredibly more difficult.

GUIDELINE 4: MONTHLY CHECK-INS

Talk to your son every month about how he's doing on the above three guidelines. This is by far your most important guideline. The 100 percent responsibility for shepherding your son falls squarely on you, Dad. Each month have a conversation about frequency, fantasy and staying connected. This routine will become normal to your son—maybe uncomfortable the first couple of times, but normal.

Your consistency about the regular check-ins will open the door to conversations about sexual issues. This should be a normal part of the father/son relationship, which should continue even if he goes away to college. I figure if every Christian man would do this check-in with his sons, we could break the curse of silence and raise the sexually healthiest sons the church and the world have seen to date.

Why? He needs to learn that male sexuality can be discussed openly and honestly with another man. He will know that he is normal sexually, and when he has sexual challenges, that sexual honesty and accountability are the solutions. This guideline alone will save your son so much potential harm. He won't feel alone in his sexuality. If he makes mistakes, you can pray together and minister to him during his sexual development. The bonding you develop can make your relationship with your son so much stronger, and he will feel that he can trust you with anything in his life.

You can do this! You're a mighty man of God who wants to bless his lineage. I am excited for you as you determine to leave a healthy sexual legacy for your family. You are the man of the house, and you will determine much of your son's sexual inheritance.

THIRTEEN

Finally,
the View!

W hen I hike in the mountainous areas of Colorado where I live, I am always grateful when I arrive at the summit and can enjoy the spectacular view. Before we get to that view, we have driven an hour or more and climbed on foot another two hours to arrive at the beautiful mountainous trail that our friends have introduced to us.

When we finally arrive at the top, the view is absolutely breathtaking. We can see for miles and feel as if we can touch the clouds. At the same time there is the feeling that nature is engulfing us to the soles of our feet. Other climbers we meet at the top of this mountain are *oohing* and *aahing* at how beautiful the view is there. During these exhilarating moments, I totally forget about the difficult climb, the aching muscles, the bruises, sweating and being hungry and thirsty. I'm simply in awe of the view and extremely grateful to be there.

Being sexually successful can be compared to enjoying this view. The intensity of your sexual life is so heightened, the intimacy so close and the afterglow so satisfying that you feel as if you have touched something extraordinary. You may already have begun to catch the view of becoming sexually successful. Just as others who have climbed before you, now you have experienced it and you can *ooh* and *aah*, too! You now can look at your wife with gratefulness and warmth.

Let's not forget that what brought us here was a strenuous climb. After reading through these pages you may realize that you have already climbed part way up the mountain to being sexually successful. We may have simply opened up a few more paths to increase your intimacy or helped to bring an increased agreement to your sexuality.

All of us have to begin the climb to sexual success from the bottom of the mountain.

Others of you have had to begin the climb to this incredible view. You may have had to retrain your dual- or multi-focused brain. Possibly you took the healing path to deal with some of the sexual distraction from past abuse, addictions or anorexia. Oh, and don't forget the valley through the issues of masturbation. Some may have needed to camp for a while through that area. Soon after came the climb to learn more about your wife, playing and learning the game of intimacy so that you can both can win.

The jaunt through the emotional-based relationships and the rocky portion through the areas of childhood, adolescence or adulthood may have been difficult terrain for you. But you persisted through it. You used your will, mind and emotions, and you scaled the cliffs that you had to overcome. If you have begun to see the view, you know why I wrote this book. It's when you see this view that absolutely takes your breath away, that you want to share it with other people.

All of us have to begin the climb to sexual success from the bottom of the mountain. The issues I presented in these chapters represent steep trails, winding valleys and cliffs that I had to climb myself. I began my journey from the valley of a multi-focused brain, sexual trauma and addiction that threatened to handicap my climb. But I chose not to make excuses. Instead I made a plan. And I have rejoiced with many men with whom I have counseled who have also chosen a plan and begun their climb to the wonderful view of sexual success.

Following a similar path that others have followed will make your journey easier. But you will still have to make the effort of the climb like the others who have arrived at the summit and are enjoying the view. You can have every bit of the sexual success for which you are willing to climb.

I wish you the absolute best on your journey toward sexual success. The day that you feel fulfilled in your sexuality with the woman you love, you'll know what the old-timers meant when they said, "There's gold in them thar hills."

GO FOR THE GOLD!

FIRST READ
MARCH 17/2004

APPENDIX A

Leviticus 18

The LORD said to Moses, "Speak to the Israelites and say to them: 'I am the LORD your God. You must not do as they do in Egypt, where you used to live, and you must not do as they do in the land of Canaan, where I am bringing you. Do not follow their practices. You must obey my laws and be careful to follow my decrees. I am the LORD your God. Keep my decrees and laws, for the man who obeys them will live by them. I am the LORD.

"'No one is to approach any close relative to have sexual relations. I am the LORD. Do not dishonor your father by having sexual relations with your mother. She is your mother; do not have relations with her.

"'Do not have sexual relations with your father's wife; that would dishonor your father. Do not have sexual relations with your sister, either your father's daughter or your mother's daughter, whether she was born in the same home or elsewhere. Do not have sexual relations with your son's daughter or your daughter's daughter; that would dishonor you.

"'Do not have sexual relations with the daughter of your father's wife, born to your father; she is your sister. Do not have sexual relations with your father's sister; she is your father's close relative. Do not have sexual relations with your mother's sister, because she is your mother's close relative. Do not dishonor your father's brother by approaching his wife to have sexual relations; she is your aunt.

"'Do not have sexual relations with your daughter-in-law. She is your son's wife; do not have relations with her. Do not have sexual relations with your brother's wife; that would dishonor your brother.

"'Do not have sexual relations with both a woman and her daughter. Do not have sexual relations with either her son's daughter or her daughter's daughter; they are her close relatives. That is wickedness.

"'Do not take your wife's sister as a rival wife and have sexual relations with her while your wife is living.

"'Do not approach a woman to have sexual relations during the uncleanness of her monthly period.

"'Do not have sexual relations with your neighbor's wife and defile yourself with her.

"'Do not give any of your children to be sacrificed to Molech, for you must not profane the name of your God. I am the LORD.

"'Do not lie with a man as one lies with a woman; that is detestable. Do not have sexual relations with an animal and defile yourself with it. A woman must not present herself to an animal to have sexual relations with it; that is a perversion.

"'Do not defile yourselves in any of these ways, because this is how the nations that I am going to drive out before you became defiled. Even the land was defiled; so I punished it for its sin, and the land vomited out its inhabitants.

"'But you must keep my decrees and my laws. The native-born and the aliens living among you must not do any of these detestable things, for all these things were done by the people who lived in the land before you, and the land became defiled. And if you defile the land, it will vomit you out as it vomited out the nations that were before you. Everyone who does any of these detestable things—such persons must be cut off from their people.

"'Keep my requirements and do not follow any of the detestable customs that were practiced before you came and do not defile yourselves with them. I am the LORD your God.'"

APPENDIX B

FEELINGS EXERCISE

1. I feel (put feeling word here) when (put a present situation when you feel this).

2. I first remember feeling (put the same feeling word here) when (explain earliest occurrence of this feeling).

Abandoned	Amused	Attractive	Breathless
Abused	Angry	Aware	Bristling
Aching	Anguished	Awestruck	Broken-up
Accepted	Annoyed	Badgered	Bruised
Accused	Anxious	Baited	Bubbly
Accepting	Apart	Bashful	Burdened
Admired	Apathetic	Battered	Burned
Adored	Apologetic	Beaten	Callous
Adventurous	Appreciated	Beautiful	Calm
Affectionate	Appreciative	Belligerent	Capable
Agony	Apprehensive	Belittled	Captivated
Alienated	Appropriate	Bereaved	Carefree
Aloof	Approved	Betrayed	Careful
Aggravated	Argumentative	Bewildered	Careless
Agreeable	Aroused	Blamed	Caring
Aggressive	Astonished	Blaming	Cautious
Alive	Assertive	Bonded	Certain
Alone	Attached	Bored	Chased
Alluring	Attacked	Bothered	Cheated
Amazed	Attentive	Brave	Cheerful

Childlike	Deprived	Foolish	Hyper
Choked-up	Deserted	Forced	Ignorant
Close	Desirable	Forceful	Ignored
Cold	Desired	Forgiven	Immature
Comfortable	Despair	Forgotten	Impatient
Comforted	Despondent	Free	Important
Competent	Destroyed	Friendly	Impotent
Competitive	Different	Frightened	Impressed
Complacent	Dirty	Frustrated	Incompetent
Complete	Disenchanted	Full	Incomplete
Confident	Disgusted	Funny	Independent
Confused	Disinterested	Furious	Insecure
Considerate	Dispirited	Gay	Innocent
Consumed	Distressed	Generous	Insignificant
Content	Distrustful	Gentle	Insincere
Cool	Distrusted	Genuine	Isolated
Courageous	Disturbed	Giddy	Inspired
Courteous	Dominated	Giving	Insulted
Coy	Domineering	Goofy	Interested
Crabby	Doomed	Grateful	Intimate
Cranky	Doubtful	Greedy	Intolerant
Crazy	Dreadful	Grief	Involved
Creative	Eager	Grim	Irate
Critical	Ecstatic	Grimy	Irrational
Criticized	Edgy	Grouchy	Irked
Cross	Edified	Grumpy	Irresponsible
Crushed	Elated	Hard	Irritable
Cuddly	Embarrassed	Harried	Irritated
Curious	Empowered	Hassled	Isolated
Cut	Empty	Healthy	Jealous
Damned	Enraged	Helpful	Jittery
Dangerous	Enraptured	Helpless	Joyous
Daring	Enthusiastic	Hesitant	Lively
Dead	Enticed	High	Lonely
Deceived	Esteemed	Hollow	Loose
Deceptive	Exasperated	Honest	Lost
Defensive	Excited	Hopeful	Loving
Delicate	Exhilarated	Hopeless	Low
Delighted	Exposed	Horrified	Lucky
Demeaned	Fake	Hostile	Lustful
Demoralized	Fascinated	Humiliated	Mad
Dependent	Feisty	Hurried	Maudlin
Depressed	Ferocious	Hurt	Malicious

Mean	Puzzled	Self-conscious	Tainted
Miserable	Quarrelsome	Separated	Tearful
Misunderstood	Queer	Sensuous	Tender
Moody	Quiet	Sexy	Tense
Morose	Raped	Shattered	Terrific
Mournful	Ravished	Shocked	Terrified
Mystified	Ravishing	Shot down	Thrilled
Nasty	Real	Shy	Ticked
Nervous	Refreshed	Sickened	Tickled
Nice	Regretful	Silly	Tight
Numb	Rejected	Sincere	Timid
Nurtured	Rejuvenated	Sinking	Tired
Nuts	Rejecting	Smart	Tolerant
Obsessed	Relaxed	Smothered	Tormented
Offended	Relieved	Smug	Torn
Open	Remarkable	Sneaky	Tortured
Ornery	Remembered	Snowed	Touched
Out of control	Removed	Soft	Trapped
Overcome	Repulsed	Solid	Tremendous
Overjoyed	Repulsive	Solitary	Tricked
Overpowered	Resentful	Sorry	Trusted
Overwhelmed	Resistant	Spacey	Trustful
Pampered	Responsible	Special	Trusting
Panicked	Responsive	Spiteful	Ugly
Paralyzed	Repressed	Spontaneous	Unacceptable
Paranoid	Respected	Squelched	Unapproachable
Patient	Restless	Starved	Unaware
Peaceful	Revolved	Stiff	Uncertain
Pensive	Riled	Stimulated	Uncomfortable
Perceptive	Rotten	Stifled	Under control
Perturbed	Ruined	Strangled	Understanding
Phony	Sad	Strong	Understood
Pleasant	Safe	Stubborn	Undesirable
Pleased	Satiated	Stuck	Unfriendly
Positive	Satisfied	Stunned	Ungrateful
Powerless	Scared	Stupid	Unified
Present	Scolded	Subdued	Unhappy
Precious	Scorned	Submissive	Unimpressed
Pressured	Scrutinized	Successful	Unsafe
Pretty	Secure	Suffocated	Unstable
Proud	Seduced	Sure	Upset
Pulled apart	Seductive	Sweet	Uptight
Put down	Self-centered	Sympathy	Used

Useful
Useless
Unworthy
Validated
Valuable
Valued
Victorious
Violated
Violent
Voluptuous
Vulnerable
Warm
Wary
Weak
Whipped
Whole
Wicked
Wild
Willing
Wiped out
Wishful
Withdrawn
Wonderful
Worried
Worthy

APPENDIX C

"Three-a-Day"

Exercise #1: Pray

David: Jesus, I thank You for a great day and for being with Ellen, the children and me. Thanks for the commission You gave me today in the job and for helping Ellen during her day. I love You, Jesus; thanks for everything.

Ellen: I too want to praise You, Jesus. You have been so good to David and me. Thank You so much for providing all that we need and so much more. You are an awesome God. Thanks for little Tony's progress in school and for Darla's new friend Jennifer; we love You, Lord.

Exercise #2: Feelings

David: I feel enthusiastic when I close a deal like I did today at the office. I first remember feeling enthusiastic when Dad would wake me up early on Saturdays when I was about six years old just to say we were going fishing.

Ellen: I feel drained after being stuck in traffic twice today. I first remember feeling drained when I was nine after being out in the snow until we were wet and cold from making snow angels.

David: I feel safe when I come home from work and I know the phone finally isn't for me. I first remember feeling safe when I was ten years old in a football league and I got to wear a real helmet and pads.

Ellen: I felt appreciated when Tony hugged me today and said you're the greatest mom. I first remember feeling appreciated when my mom made such a big deal to my dad that I cleaned my room without being told. I think I was about seven.

Exercise #3: Praise and Nurturing

David: I really appreciate you being so patient with Darla's practicing the piano every night.

Ellen: Thank you.

Ellen: I really appreciate you coming home thirty minutes early today and taking time to clean up the kitchen with me.

David: Thank you.

David: I love that you stay so attractive. Even in jeans and a T-shirt you are still so beautiful.

Ellen: Thank you.

Ellen: I love the fact that you trust my judgment in different areas of our relationship.

David: Thank you.

If you enjoyed *Sex, Men and God*, here are some other titles from Siloam Press that can help you to live in health—body, mind and spirit...

Intimacy—a 100-Day Guide to Lasting Relationships
Douglas Weiss
ISBN: 0-88419-767-0
Retail Price: $21.99

Douglas Weiss offers a 100-day practical plan that will energize your relationship and create a spiritual, emotional and physical closeness that you have hungered for in your marriage. You'll identify destructive emotional roadblocks that keep you from experiencing exciting and satisfying intimate moments with your spouse.

Breaking the Grip of Dangerous Emotions
Janet Maccaro, Ph.D., C.N.C.
ISBN: 0-88419-749-2
Retail Price: $19.99

Learn how to stop letting dangerous emotions rob you of your joy as you discover the truth about worry and stress. You can replenish your physical body with a cutting-edge nutritional program that will restore your health. Explore exciting and proven protocols for rebuilding and regenerating your body, mind and spirit.

The Coming Cancer Cure
Francisco Contreras, M.D.
ISBN: 0-88419-846-4
Retail Price: $19.99

Dr. Francisco Contreras, a leading expert in cancer treatment, writes from a world platform of experience and recognition. He says, "We are beating cancer!" He outlines the latest findings in alternative cancer research and brings new testimonials from patients who have beaten the odds. Here families will find encouragement and a practical approach to the prevention and treatment of cancer.

Living in Health—Body, Mind and Spirit

To pick up a copy of any of these titles, contact your local Christian bookstore or order online at www.siloampress.com.

Your Walk With God Can Be Even Deeper...

With *Charisma* magazine, you'll be informed and inspired by the features and stories about what the Holy Spirit is doing in the lives of believers today.

Each issue:

- Brings you exclusive world-wide reports to rejoice over.
- Keeps you informed on the latest news from a Christian perspective.
- Includes miracle-filled testimonies to build your faith.
- Gives you access to relevant teaching and exhortation from the most respected Christian leaders of our day.

Call 1-800-829-3346 for 3 FREE trial issues

Offer #A2CCHB

If you like what you see, then pay the invoice of $22.97 (**saving over 51% off the cover price**) and receive 9 more issues (12 in all). Otherwise, write "cancel" on the invoice, return it, and owe nothing.

Experience the Power of Spirit-Led Living

Charisma Offer #A2CCHB
P.O. Box 420234
Palm Coast, Florida 32142-0234
www.charismamag.com

1884A

Douglas Weiss

is the executive director of
Heart to Heart Counseling Center

4585 Hilton Parkway • Suite 202
Colorado Springs, CO 80907

P.O. Box 51055
Colorado Springs, CO 80949

719-278-3708

Telephone counseling available

3-Day Marital Intensives

www.intimatematters.com